LORD CURZON'S FAREWELL TO INDIA

Published by

Gyan Publishing House
5, Ansari Road
Daryaganj, New Delhi-110002
Phone: 011-47034999, 9811692060
E-mail: books@gyanbooks.com

Distribution Network
gyanbooks.com
India, USA, Canada, UK, Australia

ISBN: 978-93-7169-176-5 (PB)

First Published, 1907

2nd Impression 2025

Printed at: Gyan Press, Delhi.

LORD CURZON'S FAREWELL TO INDIA
Author: R. P. KARKARIA

LORD CURZON'S FAREWELL TO INDIA

BEING SPEECHES DELIVERED

AS VICEROY AND GOVERNOR-GENERAL OF INDIA,

DURING SEPT.-NOV. 1905

R. P. KARKARIA

GYAN

LORD CURZON'S FAREWELL TO INDIA.

BEING SPEECHES DELIVERED

AS VICEROY & GOVERNOR-GENERAL OF INDIA,

DURING SEPT.—NOV. 1905.

BY

THE RIGHT HONOURABLE

LORD CURZON OF KEDLESTON.

P.C., G.M.S.I., G.M.I.E., M.A., F.R.S.

TO WHICH IS ADDED

THE SPEECH AT THE PILGRIMS' DINNER:
LONDON, APRIL 1906.

EDITED WITH AN INTRODUCTION, OCCASIONAL NOTES AND ESSAYS ON CERTAIN ASPECTS OF HIS VICEROYALTY BY

R. P. KARKARIA.

"*Let India be my Judge!*"

SPEECH BEFORE BYCULLA CLUB, *p.* 14 *infra*.

"*India will become the lode-star of our memories as she has hitherto been of our duty.*"

SPEECH BEFORE UNITED SERVICE CLUB, SIMLA, *p.* 24.

"*There is not an impartial man in India, who does not know that no Englishman ever stepped on to the shores of India, who had a more passionate devotion for this country, than he who is now bidding it farewell.*"

SPEECH BEFORE BYCULLA CLUB, *p.* 13.

1907

PREFACE.

I thought that the Indian public would like to have in a permanent and separate form. the various speeches in which Lord Curzon, during the last months of his office, bade farewell to the classes and masses who compose this Indian Empire, and delighted as well as astonished them during two months last year. I am enabled to carry out the idea in the present little volume by the great kindness of Lord Curzon, to whom my thanks are in a great measure due. He was also kind enough to direct that the official text of the speeches should be supplied by the office of the Private Secretary to the Viceroy. Unfortunately this text was received too late for some of the speeches; but care has been taken to print the best available text, and to present the noble orator's words in a worthy form.

To these farewell speeches in India I have added the speech which was delivered in London at the Pilgrims' Dinner in April last, because it was akin to them, as in it also he spoke of the nature of the work that he had done in India, and also because it summed up the lessons which his high office in an Eastern Government had given him. The concluding portion of this speech is worth close attention from the democracy of England, as containing in a few weighty words the moral of his Viceroyalty in India. This speech is printed from the *Times*. to whose editor I am also indebted for the text of the beautiful poem, "Welcome," which first appeared in the columns of his paper last December.

To the gifted author of this poem. the venerable Dr. William Alexander, Archbishop of Armagh and Primate of all Ireland, my sincere thanks are due for the great kindness with which he readily acceded to my request to publish his poem here. His Grace, who is now in his eighty-third year, is very widely known as one of the best of our living sacred poets, and I am sensible of the obligation he has conferred on me by allowing his poem to appear in this volume, whose interest is much enhanced thereby.

All the speeches are given in their entirety, unabridged, and. it may be added, that some of them do not appear in the excellent selection from Lord Curzon's speeches recently published by Messrs. Macmillan. I have added the headlines and a few notes. I have also added, in the second part, a selection of such of my articles in the *Calcutta Review*, the *Times of India*, the *Madras Mail*, the *Pioneer* and elsewhere, as I thought would interest the readers of Lord Curzon's speeches. To the editors of all of them my hearty thanks are due for the permission they have kindly accorded me of reprinting them here. One of them, the Rev. Canon Saunders Dyer, sometime Archdeacon of Calcutta, has, indeed, passed beyond the reach of human thanks, while the book was passing through the press, and the Anglo-Indian literary world is decidedly the poorer by the loss of this truly gifted and pious man.

I had hoped to present this little volume, when ready, to Lady Curzon, who has left a deep impress upon the hearts of my countrymen, as Lord Curzon has undoubtedly left on our heads. But alas ! before it could be ready, she has passed beyond our reach from sunshine to the sunless land. I can now only inscribe it to her memory.

"Ah ! how soon to die !
Her quiet dream of life this hour may cease,
Her peaceful being slowly passes by
To some more perfect peace."

TARDEO, BOMBAY, R. P. KARKARIA.

12th August 1906.

CONTENTS.

(*For contents of Part II. see separate Table prefixed to that part.*)

INTRODUCTION.

Several Viceroys before Lord Curzon had bidden farewell to this country on leaving it, and a few of such speeches also attracted attention, like Lord Dufferin's memorable utterance at the St. Andrew's Dinner at Calcutta in December 1888. But none of them had bidden such an elaborate farewell to so many classes, had put so much of his heart into these speeches, had touched also the hearts of his hearers and beyond them of the vast number of his readers, as Lord Curzon. Words are but an inadequate expression at the best of what we think, and still more of what we feel. But however inadequate they may be to express all that he thought and felt in India during the last months of his stay here, they are yet significant of this fact above all others—that here India had at last found a ruler who was worthy in every way of her, sympathetic, enthusiastic, with his whole heart in the work, responsive to every chord that this country of a historic past and a bright future, so much misapprehended by friends and foes alike, can touch in his heart. Even his bitterest critics, those who have delighted to hit him below the belt, will, if they are candid, admit that if words mean anything, these speeches certainly meant a sympathy with the people of this country and an interest in their present state and future prospects, which they rarely have the good fortune to find in their rulers in anything approaching the degree they found in him. There are some passages in them which he would be a very hardened person, dead to all our finer feelings, who can read without emotion, without being sensible that he is reading the words of a man who, whatever his shortcomings may be, speaks here straight from the heart and is full of sympathy for the toiling millions of this country. One touch of nature makes the whole world kin; and there are several such touches throughout his utterances, which at once proclaim his kinship with the Indian peoples.

There is also another quality which marks these speeches, and distinguishes them from the utterances of most of his predecessors. Lord Curzon possesses imagination to a great extent, and this imagination has helped him considerably in understanding properly the people of this strange mysterious land, and in winning their regard and esteem. Indians have usually the reputation of being apathetic and irresponsive to their rulers. But Lord Curzon has shown, what was formerly known only to a few, by his career, that this apathy is much misunderstood, and that if the proper chord is touched by a master hand who instinctively knows of the secret of the Oriental mind and heart, they are not slow to respond. He was quick to seize the opportunity offered by plague and famine for this, and endeared himself by his personal presence in their midst, by making not merely ceremonial tours but real hard peregrinations throughout the country, encouraging and cheering those who were fighting these dread calamities by his own example. The imagination of the real people of India is never struck by political concessions, and those who cry out for these in their name, do them injustice, for they rarely benefit by them. What they understand and can appreciate is the alleviation of their suffering, the checking of the petty but grinding tyranny of small officials who to them represent and are the Government. By stricter supervision over such minor officials and by safeguarding the people against such tyranny as was brought to light by, among others, Sir Anthony Macdonell's Famine Commission, Lord Curzon did much more for the real people of India than would have been effected by many a political concession loudly demanded by a certain small section of educated natives. To this educated class also he has been fair and sometimes more than fair. Beyond setting his face against their demand for political privileges, which he in common with nearly all Englishmen and many of the thinking natives themselves, did not think it wise or statesman-like to grant at present, when Indians are yet in the first state of pupillage, he has done little to merit the obloquy with which he has been assailed. But as he has himself well pointed out (p. 10) this obloquy is impartially bestowed on every Viceroy during the latter part of his office, and it can do harm only to themselves. He has been the steady friend of this educated class whenever he could, compatibly with his duty to the Indians as a whole. He has, for one thing, employed them in increasing numbers in Government offices, that goal of most of this class.

Lord Curzon's rule marked a new departure in many things in Indian Administration. But in none was this more marked than in the matter of taking the people into his confidence by speeches explanatory of the policy and intentions of his Government. The Government had maintained an oracular silence more or less up to his time, broken latterly now and then by a speech on the budget in the Legislative Council from the Viceroy. This annual speech and a few others delivered on some ceremonial occasions were the sum-total of Viceregal utterance in former days. Lord Curzon boldly broke through this undue reserve, and seized every occasion of clearly expounding his policy, of explaining misunderstandings, and sometimes of refuting objections. In the eyes of some, he sometimes carried this tendency to excess. He may sometimes have been too zealous in championing his views, and may sometimes have forgotten his surroundings and imagined himself back in the House of Commons. But on the whole this policy of frank and outspoken confidence in the non-official classes both Anglo-Indian and Native, has done undoubted good, and generated trust; and nothing helps so much in governing an alien and mixed population, such as that of this country, as mutual confidence between the rulers and the ruled generated by such intercourse. Lord Curzon has set the vogue in this matter of speeches, which it would be hard for his successors not to follow. He has accustomed us to look to the head of the Government on nearly every occasion to give out the views of his Government on important matters of policy freely and frankly. And if future Heads will not do this, or do it haltingly and revert to the policy of most of his predecessors, the public will have a legitimate grievance.

Of the several individual speeches not much need be said here. Nothing has marked Lord Curzon's rule so much as the thorough and far-reaching reforms which he has peacefully initiated in the entire system of education in India. It was therefore but fitting that he should address a special farewell speech to the Directors of Public Instruction, by whose hearty co-operation he was enabled to carry out these epoch-making reforms. He was here, as he happily said, like a general, addressing his marshals for the last time before he unbuckles his sword and retires into private life. Along with the famous Resolution on educational policy issued by him on 11th March, 1904, this speech (pp. 47-57) will long be read and referred to by all those who desire to find out the principles underlying his policy in this important subject in all its various branches. He has begun a movement which we may well call with him the renaissance of education in India ; and if it is properly kept up by his successors, it will fulfill all his best hopes.

On one particular branch of education in which he had interested himself deeply, that of the proper training of the sons of Native Chiefs and Princes, on which much of the future of Native States depends, Lord Curzon took occasion to speak specially at his farewell speech at the Daly Chiefs' College, at Indore (pp. 40-46). Therein he has clearly announced the policy of Government towards such Chiefs' Colleges, and urged emphatically on old-fashioned Sirdars and Thakors the indispensable necessity of bringing up their sons in modern ways. The education of the people and the princes, of the ryat as well as the Raja, ought clearly to proceed hand in hand. Education ought not to be the monopoly, as it has been practically in the immediate past, of a small section of the middle class, which has done so much to reduce unnaturally the weight that is their due in the politics of the country of these princes and peasants. The farewell message to the Indian Princes which this speech contains (p. 42) shows the cordial nature of his relations with the Native Princes of India, and his anxious solicitude during his rule that they should exert that weight and influence in all matters relating not only to their States but also in Imperial Councils, which is clearly their due. This subject of the relation of Native Princes with the paramount power he also handled in his speech (pp. 36-39) on the installation of the Maharajah of Kashmir, a thoroughly loyal ward of the British, and one specially deserving of their protection, as he holds the state of Kashmir as a free gift granted to his grandfather Golab Sing less than sixty years ago by the English. The occasion was indeed unique, for it was the first instance in the entire history of English relations with the feudatory States of the conferring of an enhancement or restitution of powers on a Native Prince. It is by such speeches, mingling advice with encouragement, that Lord Curzon has succeeded in winning the confidence of these Princes and States; which, in the present position of the country, ought to be a valuable asset of the Indian Empire, making for stability as against the noisy discontent and unrest manifested by the small educated class.

It was Lord Curzon's good fortune throughout the seven years of his labours in this country to receive the hearty and zealous support and co-operation of all his colleagues in the administration of both the Civil and Military Services. He well knew that to this co-operation was due in a great measure the success with which his efforts had been crowned, despite the strong prejudice which a reforming Viceroy always excites. Lord Curzon ran many a time counter to the vested interests and prejudices of the great Services. It is therefore very creditable to them that they should have worked with him with a will to make his administration such a brilliant success. All this Lord Curzon sought a special opportunity to acknowledge, and such an opportunity was given him by the United Service Club at Simla. The splendid eulogium which he has there pronounced on his colleagues and lieutenants (pp. 16-22) is worthy of the speaker and still more of the recipients. The Indian Services, especially the Civil Service, have been the honoured recipients of praise by several distinguished *laudatis viris*, and among these they will no doubt value very highly the well weighed words of studied praise pronounced deliberately by Lord Curzon. They are fully worthy to rank by the side of these memorable words uttered by that philosopher-statesman, Sir Henry Maine, a little before his death as the deliberate opinion of a long life spent in the service of India both here and at home. "The 'Indian Bureaucracy' is merely a barbarous foreign phrase applied with gross inaccuracy to as remarkable a group of public servants as any country has produced, engaged in administering the affairs of a vast population under perfectly definite and intelligibly stated rules. If Government be an art an 'Old Indian' is constantly a man who has practised it with more success and under far more difficulties than the foremost English statesman." (Sir H. Maine, in Ward's *Reign of Victoria*, Vol. I. p. 524, 1887).

At the present time, when we are all reading Mr. John Morley's notable recent Budget speech, and his words,—"he had met Military Officers and men who were described as 'sun-dried bureaucrats,' and he had discovered that the 'sun-dried bureaucrat' was a man eminent for his experience, knowledge and responsibility faithfully and honourably discharged."—are ringing in our ears, we are forcibly reminded of the words of Lord Curzon uttered ten months ago. No three more eminent men, eminent as statesmen as well as men of letters and thought, could be found among Englishmen than Maine, Mr. Morley and Lord Curzon, and when they unite in praising Indian administrators, it is surely presumptuous in far lesser men to prate about "sun-dried bureaucrats."

Nor did the higher services alone monopolise Lord Curzon's attention or his praise. It was quite characteristic of him that he should not forget the humble clerks who work day and night in the various Secretariats, those silent, unseen and therefore unappreciated workmen, underground as it were, who send up baskets of ore from which others make their gold and name and fame. It illustrates the qualities of imaginativeness and sympathy above referred to, that Lord Curzon should have bestowed a thought on these men during his last crowded and busy days at Simla, and have set apart an hour to address to them a singularly touching little speech (pp. 25-26). The speech is thoroughly characteristic of the man, who ruled over the hearts of men with a heart of his own; and words like the following explain the secret of his popularity with the masses of the people of India which no amount of obloquy raised by a certain class of critics has been able to cloud from our sight: "As the final court of appeal on every case, great or small, amid the vast population of India, a Viceroy has chances that occur to but few. I think that he ought to take them. I have tried to do so. I can recall long night hours, spent in the effort to unravel some tangled case of alleged misconduct resulting in the dismissal of a poor unknown native subordinate. Perhaps those hours have not been the worst spent of my time in India, and the simple letters of gratitude from the score of more of humble individuals whom I have thus saved from ruin have been equally precious in my eyes with the resolutions of public bodies or the compliments of princes." (p. 26).

The Coronation Durbar held at Delhi in 1903, was a grand event in Lord Curzon's rule, and that city, as well as its sister of Agra, appealed specially to the historic imagination with which he is gifted in an eminent degree. The short speeches (pp. 32-35) which he delivered to the citizens of both these cities, fitly allude to the work of archæological restoration, which he had begun in India, wherever there were ancient monuments to be preserved, but which he personally supervised in those imperial cities of the Moguls, so full of renowned architectural buildings that had fallen into ruin. The Punjab felt itself somewhat humiliated during Lord Curzon's rule, because he had carved out the North-West Frontier Province chiefly from its territories, and placed it under a separate administration directly under the Government of India. Its *amour propre* must have been somewhat appeased by the Coronation Durbar being held within its province at Delhi. Lord Curzon further propitiated it by making a short farewell speech (pp. 30-31) at Lahore, its capital.

But the best speech was reserved, as was but fitting, for Bombay, the first city in India in name as well as reality, though not its capital. Bombay had perhaps of all Indian cities watched Lord Curzon's rule most keenly, and partly from its position at a distance viewed it in proper perspective. Partly on account of the sobriety which always distinguishes its political activity, and partly on account of the strong leaven of Anglo-Indian society which prevails here much to its benefit, Bombay has been able to do the retiring Viceroy greater justice than other cities and provinces. Here the famous Byculla Club, which is proud to receive Viceroys and other great Indian statesmen and citizens as its guests, set the hall-mark of its approval on Lord Curzon's work in India, and entertained him at a magnificent banquet. The approval of this Club meant not only that of the large and very influential Anglo-Indian public, but also, beyond that, of a great part of the native public, especially the mercantile, trading and landowning classes. Hence, in his speech before this Club, Lord Curzon was truly speaking before the whole Indian public, and not as in his preceding farewell speeches, before this or that class or certain sections of the public, however exalted. Here he touched the high-water mark of his oratorical powers. It is not an *apologia pro regno suo*, as some have supposed; it is not even a vindication : he was too conscious of the dignity of his high office ever to attempt that. It was a clear exposition, candid and manly, of the principles that ever were present before his mind's eye and that guided his policy throughout. He had, indeed, disclosed those principles piecemeal on former occasions throughout his career here, whenever he had an opportunity for so doing—and indeed, as we have said before, his Viceroyalty is marked by nothing so much as this characteristic of taking the people into his confidence by frank outspoken utterance. But here we have them all, and we are shewn in a masterly way their application in all departments of state. And all this is done with consummate skill, and over it all breathes an earnestness that would extort admiration even from professed and determined opponents. From a person who was so wilfully and bitterly criticised, it would have been expected that he would have been at least to some extent bitter, especially as it was the last occasion when he could speak with the authority of a Viceroy. But there is not a word of bitterness, nothing in the tone to which his bitterest critic could take exception. In the speaker there stands truly revealed the man, magnanimous, tender-hearted, sympathising with the sorrows of the famine-stricken peasant, the impoverished luckless ryot, and the plague-stricken inhabitant of towns. He has the satisfaction of having done as much as a single ruler can do to alleviate, in however small a degree, the woes of the poor population of India. And what is more, the poor of this land know and appreciate it as far as they can know and appreciate such work at all.

WELCOME.

Thou, who the grandest crown hast taken off
With thine own hand, our first of men can wear,
O full of toil beyond the taunt of scoff,

Welcome, high welcome, to our wintry air—
Full well our English instinct knows a man;
What worthy wreath of words shall we prepare?

Not lights of speech and flowers—what all may scan—
Some words of thee well-loved, majestic, calm,
Of an august simplicity that can

Outlive all our comparison—a psalm,
Whose life is told by thousands of our years
Heaven-high, yet full of home's familiar balm.

So to our race in India full and strong
Fell from thy lips that phrase no time outwears,
"Thou hast loved righteousness and hated wrong"—

Thus spake our great men of the olden time,
Who grandly spoke, because they grandly thought—
Whose spirit first, then speech, became sublime!

Colossal brevity as by magic wrought,
Catching the difficult ear of after time;
Restraint—and not effusion—dearly bought

Now, when our politic armies in their place
Stand clamouring by the fires along their line,
Each battle sees the other's angry face,

Come now with utterance of the men of old,
Come thou, be judged of all this land of thine—
Not with a pomp of colour and of gold;

Thy speech is not like those who fain would try
Moonbeams through glass—a lovely impotence,
Lustrous but lifeless, fading firelessly;

Thou who has instinct of a mighty work,
Of the great utterance of the days gone by.
Superb as Chatham, steadfast-souled as Burke.

WILLIAM ARMAGH.

[In this poem which the Most Reverend Dr. William Alexander, Archbishop of Armagh and Primate of all Ireland contributed to the *Times* on Monday, December 4, on Lord Curzon's return to England, and which is here reproduced by His Grace's kind permission, and that of the Editor of the *Times*, reference is made to the quotation from the Psalms xlv., 7, and Hebrews i. 9, in the farewell speech at the Byculla Club.]

SPEECH AT THE BYCULLA CLUB.

On Thursday November 16th, Lord Curzon was entertained at dinner by the Byculla Club, Bombay. Their Excellencies the Governors of Bombay and of Madras. Lord Lamington and Lord Ampthill, were also present. Mr. Leslie Crawford, President of the Club, having proposed his health in felicitous terms, Lord Curzon replied in the following speech, in which his great oratorical powers may be said to have worthily culminated :—

Mr. President, Your Excellencies and Gentlemen,—Three times have the Byculla Club honoured me with an invitation to dinner. The first occasion was when I was leaving India at the end of my first term of office in April 1904. The second was when I returned to India for my second term in December, 1904; and this is the third, when I am finally departing. I have esteemed this triple compliment most highly. For ordinarily Bombay does not see or know much of the Viceroy except what it reads in the newspapers, which is not perhaps uniformly favourable; and, with a Governor of your own, you cannot be expected to take as much interest in the head of the Supreme Government as other communities or places with which he is brought into more frequent contact. In respect of Bombay, however, I have been unusually fortunate in my time, for apart from the four occasions of arrival or departure, I have been here once in Lord Sandhurst's and once in Lord Northcote's time, and again a week ago, so that this is my seventh visit in seven years. Here I made my first speech on Indian shores and here it is not unfitting that I should make my last. Calcutta did me the honour of inviting me to a parting banquet, and so did the Civil Service of Bengal, and I was greatly touched by those compliments. But I felt that, having accepted your invitation, I owed a duty to you, and that I should only become a nuisance if I allowed myself either the luxury or the regret of too many farewells.

Gentleman, it is no exaggeration to say that my several visits to this city have given me an unusual interest in its fortunes. I have seen it in prosperity and I have seen it in suffering; and I have always been greatly struck by the spirit and patriotism of its citizens. There seems to me to be here an excellent feeling between the very different races and creeds. Bombay possesses an exceptional number of public-spirited citizens, and the sense of civic duty is as highly developed as in any great city that I know. If there is a big movement afoot, you lend yourselves to it with a powerful and concentrated will and a united Bombay is not a force to be gainsaid. Let me give as an illustration the magnificent success of your reception and entertainment of T. R. H. the Prince and Princess of Wales. Moreover, you have the advantage of one of the best conducted and ablest newspapers in Asia. My recollections of Bombay are also those of uniform kindness towards myself, a kindness which has found active expression on each occasion that I have visited the city, and that has culminated to-night in this splendid entertainment and in the reception that you have just accorded to my health.

As to the speech of the Chairman, to which we listened just now, I hardly feel that I know what I ought to say. He seemed to me to be so familiar with all the details of my administration that I felt that if I ever wanted a biographer it is to Bombay and to the Byculla Club that I must come to find him. But his account of what I have done—or perhaps I should rather say endeavoured to do—was characterised by so generous an insistence on the best, that I almost felt that a rival orator should be engaged to get up and paint the opposite side of the picture. I know of several who would have been prepared without a gratuity to undertake the congenial task—only in that case I should not perhaps have enjoyed the hospitality of this gathering! I must therefore leave things as they are, and content myself with thanking the Chairman for his great and undeserved kindness in his treatment of the subject of his toast. Gentlemen, I have thus endeavoured to express my acknowledgments of your kindness, and I must include in these acknowledgments those of Lady Curzon. Your gracious reference to her presence greatly touched my heart.

Gentlemen, I have expressed my acknowledgment of your kindness. May I also take this opportunity through you of thanking all those communities and persons who, from all parts of India, have, during the past three months, showered upon me expressions of esteem and regret? I think I am justified in assuming, both from the quarters from which they have emanated and also from the language employed, that these have not been merely conventional expressions. From a departing Viceroy no one in India has anything more to ask or to expect; his sun is setting, and another orb is rising above the horizon. If in these circumstances, from representative bodies and associations, from the leaders of races and communities, from princes, and from unknown humble men, such messages, couched in such unaffected language as have crowded in upon me, while he cannot but feel very grateful for all this kindness, there may also steal into his mind the comforting reflection that he has not altogether laboured in vain, but has perhaps left some footprints that will not be washed out by the incoming tide.

Gentlemen, it is almost seven years ago that I stood upon the neighbouring quay on the morning that I landed to take up my new office. Well do I remember the occasion and the scene: the Bunder gay with bunting and brilliant with colour; the background of the acclaiming streets with their tens of thousands, and the setting of the stateliest panorama in Asia. I do not deny that to me it was a very solemn moment, for I was coming here to take up the dream of my life and to translate into fact my higher aspirations. In that spirit I endeavoured to respond to the address of the Corporation, and were I landing again tomorrow,

I would use the same language again. Oceans seem now to roll between that day and this ; oceans of incident and experience, of zest and achievement, of anxiety and suffering, of pleasure and pain. But as I stood there that morning and the vista spread out before me, I said that I came to India to hold the scales even, and as I stand here to-night seven years later, I dare to say in all humility that I have done it—have held the scales even between all classes and all creeds—sometimes to my detriment, often at a cost that none but myself can tell, but always with such truth and fidelity as in me lay. I further said that the time for judgment was not when a man puts on his armour but when he takes it off. Even now I am fast unbuckling mine, in a few hours the last piece will have been laid aside. But, gentlemen, the test. Can I survive my own test? The answer to that I must leave to you among many others, and by your verdict I am willing to abide.

Gentlemen, when I came here seven years ago, I had some idea, but not perhaps a very complete idea, of what the post of Viceroy of India is. Now that I am in a position to give a more matured opinion on the subject, I may proceed to throw a little light upon it. There are, I believe, many people at home who cherish the idea that the Viceroy in India is the representative of the Sovereign, in much the same way as Viceroys or Governors-General in other parts of the British Empire, except that India being in the East, it is considered wise to surround him with peculiar state and ceremonial, while in a country which is not a constitutional colony but a dependency, it is of course necessary to invest him with certain administrative powers. No conception of the Viceroy's position and duties could well be wider of the mark. Certainly the proudest and most honourable of his functions is to act as representative of the Sovereign, and this fact is invested with unusual solemnity and importance in a society organised like that of India upon the aristocratic basis, where the Throne is enveloped in an awe that is the offspring of centuries, and is supported by princely dynasties in many cases as old as itself. The consciousness of this responsibility should, I think, always act both as a stimulus and as a check to the Viceroy,—a stimulus to him to act in a manner worthy of the exalted station in which for a short time he is placed, and a check to keep him from inconsiderate or unworthy deeds. But that is of course only the beginning of the matter. The Viceroy very soon finds out that the purely Viceregal aspect of his duties is the very least portion of them, and the Court-life in which he is commonly depicted by ignorant people as revelling, occupies only the place of a compulsory background in his everyday existence. He soon discovers that he is the responsible head of what is by far the most perfected and considerable of highly organised Governments in the world ; for the Government of China, which is supposed to rule over a larger number of human beings, can certainly not be accused of a high level of either organisation or perfection. So much is the Viceroy the head of that Government that almost every act of his subordinates is attributed to him by public opinion ; and if he is of an active and enterprising nature, a sparrow can scarcely twitter its tail at Peshawar without a response being detected to masterful orders from Simla or Calcutta. This aspect of the Viceroy's position makes him the target of public criticism to a degree in excess, I think, of that known in any foreign country, except perhaps America. I think that in India, this is sometimes carried too far. When the Viceroy speaks, he is supposed to remember only that he is the representative of the Sovereign. But when he is spoken or written about it is commonly only as head of the adminstration, and then nothing is sometimes too bad for him. I only make these remarks because this seems to me rather a one-sided arrangement, and, because I think anything to be deprecated that might deter your Viceroys from taking the supreme and active part in administration which it seems to me to be their duty to do. You do not want them to be figureheads. You want them to pull the stroke oar in the boat. You want English Ministries to send you their very best men, and then you want to get out of them not the correct performance of ceremonial duties, but the very best work of which their energies or experiences or abilities may render them capable. Anything, therefore, that may deter them from such a conception of their duties or confine them to the sterile pursuit of routine is, in my view, greatly to be deplored.

However, I am only yet at the beginning of my enumeration of the Viceroy's tale of bricks. He is the head, not merely of the whole Government, but also of the most arduous department of Government, namely, the Foreign Office. There he is in the exact position of an ordinary Member of Council, with the difference that the work of the Foreign Department is unusually responsible, and that it embraces three spheres of action so entirely different and requiring such an opposite equipment of principles and knowledge, as the conduct of relations with the whole of the Native States of India, the management of the frontier provinces and handling of the frontier tribes, and the offering of advice to his Majesty's Government on practically the entire foreign policy of Asia, which mainly or wholly concerns Great Britain in its relation to India. But the Viceroy, though he is directly responsible for this one Department is scarcely less responsible for the remaining. He exercises over them a control which is, in my judgment, the secret of efficient administration. It is the counterpart of what used to exist in England, but has died out since the days of Sir Robert Peel—with consequences which cannot be too greatly deplored. I earnestly hope that the Viceroy in India may never cease to be head of the Government in the fullest sense of the term. It is not one man's rule, which may or may not be a good thing—that depends on the man. But it is one man's supervision, which is the very best form of Government, presuming the man to be competent. The alternative in India is bureaucracy, which is the most mechanical and lifeless of all forms of administration.

To continue, the Viceroy is also the President of the Legislative Council, where he has to defend the policy of Government in speeches which are apt to be denounced as empty, if they indulge in platitudes, and as undignified, if they do not. He must have a financial policy, an agricultural policy, a famine policy, a plague policy, a railway policy, an educational policy, an industrial policy, a military policy. Every body in the country who has a fad or a grievance, and how many are there without either, hunts him out. Every public servant who wants an increase of pay,allowances, or pension—a not inconsiderable band—appeals to him as the eye of justice; everyone who thinks he deserves recognition, appeals to him as the fountain of honour. When he goes on tour he has to try to know nearly as much about local needs as the people who have lived there all their lives, and he has to refuse vain requests in a manner to make the people who asked them feel happier than they were before. When he meets the merchants he must know all about tea, sugar, indigo, jute, cotton, salt and oil. He is not thought much of unless he can throw in some knowledge of shipping and customs. In some places electricity, steel, and iron and coal are required. For telegraphs, he is supposed to have a special partiality; and is liable to be attacked about the metric system. He must be equally prepared to discourse about labour in South Africa or labour in Assam. The connecting link between him and Municipalities is supplied by water and drains. He must be prepared to speak about everything and often about nothing. He is expected to preserve temples, to keep the currency steady, to satisfy third class passengers, to patronise race meetings, to make Bombay and Calcutta each think that it is the capital city of India, and to purify the police. He corresponds with all his lieutenants in every province, and it is his duty to keep in touch with every Local Administration. If he does not reform everything that is wrong, he is told that he is doing too little, if he reforms anything at all, that he is doing too much.

I am sure that I could occupy quite another five minutes of your time in depicting the duties which you require of the Viceroy in India, and to which I might have added the agreeable finale of being entertained at complimentary banquets. But I have said enough perhaps to show that it is no light burden that I am now laying down and that it is not perhaps surprising if seven years of it should prove enough for any average constitution. And yet I desire to say on this parting occasion that I regard the office of Viceroy of India, inconceivably laborious as it is, as the noblest office in the gift of the British Crown. I think the man who does not thrill upon receiving it with a sense not of foolish pride but of grave responsibility, is not fit to be an Englishman. I believe that the man who holds it with devotion and knows how to wield the power wisely and well, as so many great men in India have done, can for a few years exercise a greater influence upon the destinies of a larger number of his fellow creatures than any head of an Administration in the Universe. I hold that England ought to send out to India to fill this great post the pick of her statesmen, and that it should be regarded as one of the supreme prizes of an Englishman's career. I deprecate any attempt, should it ever be made, to attenuate its influence, to diminish its privileges, or to lower its prestige. Should the day ever come when the Viceroy of India is treated as the mere puppet or mouthpiece of the Home Government, who is required only to carry out whatever orders it may be thought desirable to transmit, I think that the justification for the post would have ceased to exist. But I cannot believe that the administrative wisdom of my countrymen, which is very great, would ever tolerate so great a blunder.

And now, Gentlemen, after this little sketch of the duties of a Viceroy, you may expect to hear something of the manner of fulfilling them. I have been told that on the present occasion I am expected to give a sort of synopsis of the last seven years of administration. I am sure you will be intensely relieved to learn that I intend to disappoint those expectations. List of laws, or administrative acts, or executive policies, may properly figure in a budget speech; they may be recorded in an official Minute, they may be grouped and weighed by the historian. But they are hardly the material for an after-dinner oration. Besides which I have been spared the necessity of any such review by the generous ability with which it has already been performed for me by the press.

Inasmuch, however, as all policy that is deserving of the name must rest upon certain principles, perhaps you will permit me to point out what are the main principles that have underlain everything to which I have set my hand in India. They are four in number. The first may sound very elementary, but it is in reality cardinal. It is the recognition that for every department of the State, and for every branch of the administration, there must be a policy instead of no policy, that is a method of treating the subject in question which is based upon accepted premises, either of reasoning or experience, and is laid down in clear language, understood by the officers who have to apply it, and intelligible to the people to whom it is to be applied. It is in fact the negation of a policy of drift.

Years ago I remember coming to India and commencing my studies on the Frontier Question. I enquired of everyone I met what was the Frontier Policy of the Government of India. I even mounted as high as Members of Council. No one could tell me. I found one view at Calcutta, another at Lahore, another at Peshawar, and another at Quetta, and scores of intervening shades between. That is only an illustration; but that absence of a policy cost India thousands of lives and crores of rupees. Of course, in our attempt to fashion or to formulate policies my colleagues and I may not always have been successful—our policy need not have been uniformly right. We make no such claim. All that we say is that the policy is now there, not hidden away or enshrouded in hieroglyphics, but practically laid down, in most cases already given to the world, and in every case available for immediate use. There is not a single branch of the administration, internal or external, of which I believe that this cannot truthfully be said. I will give you a few illustrations drawn from spheres as widely separated as possible.

Take Foreign Affairs. The Government of India can hardly be described as having a Foreign Policy of their own, because our foreign relations must necessarily be co-ordinated with those of the Empire. But we can have our views and can state them for what they are worth; and there are certain countries in the close neighbourhood of our frontiers where the conduct of affairs is necessarily in our hands. Thus, in respect of Tibet the Government of India have throughout had a most definite policy which has not perhaps been fully understood, because it has never been fully stated in published correspondence, but which I have not the slightest doubt will vindicate itself, and that before long. Similarly with regard to Afghanistan, our policy throughout my term of office has been directed to clearing up all the doubt or misunderstandings that had arisen out of our different agreements with the late Amir, and to a renewal of those agreements, freed from such ambiguity, with his successor. Itwas to clear all these doubts that the Mission was sent to Kabul, as the Amir found himself unable to carry out his first intention to come down to India; and for all the widespread tales that the Mission had been sent to press roads or railroads or telegraphs and all sorts of unacceptable conditions upon the Amir from which the Government of India or myself was alleged to have been only with difficulty restrained by a cautious Home Government, there was never one shred of foundation.

Perhaps in Persia, a subject which is perhaps better appreciated and is certainly better written about in Bombay than in any other city of the Empire, we have been able to do most in respect of a positive and intelligible policy. Resting upon Lord Lansdowne's statesmanlike and invaluable dictum as to the Persian Gulf, from which I trust that no British Government will ever be so foolish as to recede, we have been able to pursue a definite course of action in defence of British interests at Muscat, Bahrein, Koweit, and throughout the Persian Gulf. The same applies to Mekran and Seistan, and I believe that I leave British interests in those quarters better safeguarded than they have ever before been. I will not trouble you further about Foreign affairs to-night—though I might take you round the confines of the Indian Empire and show you an Aden Boundary determined, largely owing to the ability of the officers serving under my noble friend [Lord Lamington], our relations with Sikkim and Bhutan greatly strengthened, and the final settlement of the China-Burmese boundary practically achieved.

Neither will I detain you about the tribal frontier of India, although the fact that I can dismiss this almost in a sentence is perhaps more eloquent than any speech could be. The point is that the Government of India, the local officers, and the tribesmen now know exactly what we are aiming at, namely, in so far as we are obliged to maintain order, to keep up communications, or to exert influence in the tribal area, to do it, not with British troops but through the tribes themselves. The other day I saw the Chief Commissioner of the North-West Frontier Province, and asked him if he could sum up the position on the Frontier. 'Yes', he replied, 'I can, in a single word, and that is "Confidence."' Confidence at Hunza, confidence at Chitral,—which, when I came out to India, I was told by the *pundits* at home that I should have to evacuate in a year, but which is now as tranquil as the compound of the Byculla Club,—confidence in the Khyber and the Kurram, confidence all down the frontier of Baluchistan. Gentlemen, that is no mean boast. I observe that all the persons, who have for years depicted me as a somewhat dangerous person, and who were kind enough to warn India seven years ago of the terrible frontier convulsions that she was in for under my rule, have found it a little difficult to account for the seven years' peace that has settled down on the land. Two explanations have, however, lately been forthcoming. The first is that the tribes were so severely handled by my predecessor that they have not had a kick in them left for me. The second is that having concentrated all my unholy propensities in the direction of Tibet, where, however, for some unexplained reason I did not begin until I had been in India for four years, I had nothing left for the tribes. I do not think that I need be disturbed by either of these criticisms. I can hand over the frontier to my successor, with the happy assurance not only that matters are quiet, but that the principles determining our action, whether as regards tribal militia, or border military police, or frontier roads and railways, or tribal control, are all clearly laid down, and are understood. If these principles are departed from, if the Government of India were to go on for a policy of cupidity or adventure, then the confidence of which I have spoken would not last a month. Otherwise I do not see why it should not be enduring.

We have also for seven years pursued a very consistent military policy, nor differing therein in the least from the distinguished men who preceeded us, but using the much larger opportunities that have been presented to us by recurring surpluses to carry out measures of which they often dreamed, but which they had not the funds to realise. I am not one of those who think that the Indian Army is a bad one. I believe it to be by far the best portion of the forces of the British Crown: and certainly such work as it has been my duty to ask it to undertake, whether in South Africa or China or Somaliland or Tibet has been as good as any in the history of the Empire. We have done a good deal to render the Indian Army, I will not say more efficient, but more effective. We have entirely re-armed every section of it. We have reorganised the horse and field artillery from top to bottom. We have created a new transport organisation, we are now making our own gunpowder, rifles, gun-carriages and guns; we have added 580 British officers and are proposing to add 350 more, we are doubling the Native Army reserves—and all these measures are independent of the schemes of reorganisation and redistribution of which you have heard so much. If due attention continues to be paid to the idiosyncrasies of the Native Army, and if it is treated sympathetically, I believe that we shall continue to receive from it the splendid level of service which is its tradition and its glory.

In the sphere of internal politics we have adopted a slightly different method, though with the same end, for there we have as a rule not framed our policy without a most exhaustive preliminary examination of the data upon which it ought to rest conducted by the most expert authorities whose services we could command. Thus we did not proceed to draw up a plague policy until the Plague Commission had reported. Our new Famine Code and Manuals, the methods by which the Government of India will grapple with the next famine when it comes, and the preventive methods which we have been bringing into operation one by one are the results of the Commission over which Sir Antony MacDonnell presided. The great programme of Irrigation schemes for the whole of India to which we have committed ourselves, at a cost of thirty millions sterling in twenty years, was similarly not arrived at until Sir Colin Moncreiff's Commission had spent two winters in India. I did not undertake University reform until I had carefully sifted the facts of the case by a Commission upon which the highest authorities had seats. Nor did we charge ourselves with the reform of the Police until we had conducted a most searching enquiry into the facts of existing administration in every Province by Sir Andrew Fraser's Commission. Finally, we did not propose to create a Railway Board or to revolutionise our railway management until we had obtained the advice of an expert from home. Thus, wherever possible, we have proceeded upon the same plan: first, the ascertainment from the information at our disposal, from the representations of the public, and from the known facts, that there was a case for reform; secondly, the appointment of an influential and representative body to go round the country and take evidence; thirdly, the critical examination of their report, accompanied by consultation of Local Governments and of public opinion; fourthly, the accomplished reform. I remember very well—I dare say you do also, gentlemen,—when the present administration was ridiculed as one of Commissions that were always sitting but whose egg never hatched out. I held my peace, but I sat all the harder. Time was all I wanted; and now I can say that not a single Commission has sat and reported in my time without its results having been embodied with the least possible delay in administrative measures or in legislative Acts. If you want to know the Educational Policy of Government you can find it in the published Resolution of March 1904. I recapitulated it in a recent farewell speech at Simla. If you want to know our Land Revenue Policy, it is similarly enunciated in two published Resolutions dealing with the principle of assessment and collection, which will presently be followed by two others dealing with subsidiary branches of the question. These will then be a corpus or Code of Land Revenue law and policy, such as has never previously existed in India, and which will constitute a charter for the cultivating classes. If you want to know our Fiscal Policy it is contained in the published Despatch of October 1903. Thus wherever you turn, I think you will find my claim justified,—the case examined, the principles elucidated, the policy laid down, action taken and already bearing fruit.

The second principle that I have held in view has been this. Amid the numerous races and creeds of whom India is composed, while I have sought to understand the needs and to espouse the interests of each, to win the confidence of the Princes, to encourage and strengthen the territorial aristocracy, to provide for the better education and thus to increase the opportunities of the educated classes, to stimulate the energies of Hindu, Mahomedan, Buddhist, and Sikh, and to befriend those classes like the Eurasians who are not so powerful as to have many friends of their own—my eye has always rested upon a larger canvas, crowded with untold numbers, the real people of India, as distinct from any class or section of the people—

> "But thy poor endure
> And are with us yet;
> Be thy name a sure
> Refuge for thy poor,
> Whom men's eyes forget."

It is the Indian poor, the Indian peasant, the patient, humble, silent millions, the eighty per cent, who subsist by agriculture, who know very little of policies, but who profit or suffer by their results, and whom men's eyes, even the eyes of their own countrymen too often forget—to whom I refer. He has been in the background of every policy for which I have been responsible, of every surplus of which I have assisted in the disposition. We see him not in the splendour and opulence, nor even in the squalor, of great cities: he reads no newspapers, for, as a rule, he cannot read at all: he has no politics. But he is the bone and sinew of the country, by the sweat of his brow the soil is tilled, from his labour comes forth the national income: he should be the first and final object of every Viceroy's regard.

It is for him in the main that we have twice reduced the salt tax, that we remitted land revenue in two years amounting to nearly two and a half millions sterling: for him that we are assessing the land revenue at a progressively lower pitch and making its collection elastic. It is to improve his credit that we have created co-operative credit societies, so that he may acquire capital at easy rates and be saved from the usury of the money-lender. He is the man whom we desire to lift in the world, to whose children we want to give education, to rescue whom from tyranny and oppression we have reformed the Indian Police, and from whose cabin we want to ward off penury and famine. Above all let us keep him on the soil and rescue him from bondage or expropriation. When I am vituperated by those who claim to speak for the Indian people, I feel no resentment and no pain. For I search my conscience and I ask myself who and what are the real Indian people; and I rejoice that it has fallen to my lot to do something to alleviate theirs, and that I leave them better than I found them. As for the educated classes, I regret if because I have not extended to them political concessions—more places on councils and so on,—I have in any way incurred their hostility. For I certainly in no wise return it; and when I remember how impartially it is bestowed on every Viceroy in the latter part of his term of office, I conclude that there must be something wrong about all of us which brings us under a common ban. I also remember that in a multitude of ways, even as regards places and appointments, I have consistently befriended and championed their cause. I have not offered political concessions, because I did not regard it as wisdom or statesmanship in the interest of India itself to do so ; and if I have incurred odium for thus doing my duty I have no apology to advance.

And yet in one respect I venture to think that the classes of whom I am speaking have found in me their best friend. For I have endeavoured to pursue with them the third principle of action to which I before alluded, namely to be frank and outspoken, to take them into open confidence as to the views and intentions of Government, to profit by public opinion instead of ignoring it, never to flatter or cozen and never to mystify or deceive. I have always held that Governors are servants of the public, and that policies are not such high and holy things as not to admit of clear exposition and candid argument for all who care to hear. I cannot say that I have everywhere been rewarded for this confidence. But I have pursued it as part of a definite policy, for there has not been an act or an aim of Government whose sincerity I have not been prepared to vindicate, and to me there is something manlier in treating your critics with respect than in pretending that you are unaware even of their existence. And my last principle, Gentlemen, has been everywhere to look ahead ; to scrutinize not merely the passing requirements of the hour, but the abiding needs of the country, and to build not for the present alone but for the future. I should say that the one great fault of Englishmen in India is that we do not sufficiently look ahead. We are so much absorbed in the toil of the day that we leave the morrow to take care of itself. But it is not to-morrow only but twenty years hence, fifty years hence, a hundred years hence. That is the thought that has never left my mind. I have had no ambition to cut Gordian knots or to win ephemeral triumphs. I am content that all my work should go that is not fitted to last. Some of it will go of course. But I hope that a solid residuum may remain and take its place as part of the organic growth of Indian politics and Indian society. To leave India permanently stronger and more prosperous, to have added to the elements of stability in the national existence, to have cut out some sources of impurity or corruption, to have made out dispositions that will raise the level of administration not for a year or two but continuously, to have lifted the people a few grades in the scale of well being, to have enabled the country or the Government better to confront the dangers or the vicissitudes of the future—that is the statesman's ambition. Whether he has attained it or not, will perhaps not be known until long after he has disappeared.

I need say but few words about my resignation or the causes that led to it. I desire only to mention one cause that did not. It seems to have been thought in some quarters at home that this was a personal quarrel, and that I resigned on personal grounds. No one who has the least acquaintance with the facts of the case, and I would fain hope to one who has any acquaintance with myself, could commit this error. The post of Viceroy of India is not one which any man fit to hold it would resign for any but the strongest reasons. When you remember that to me it was the dream of my childhood, the fulfilled ambition of my manhood, and my highest conception of duty to the State, when further you remember that I was filling it for the second time, a distinction which I valued much less for the compliment than for the opportunity afforded to me of completing the work to which I had given all the best of my life, you may judge whether I should be likely heedlessly or impulsively to lay it down. No, Sir, there is not a man in this room who does not know that I resigned for a great principle, or rather for two great principles: first, the hitherto uncontested, the essential, and in the long run the indestructible subordination of military to civil authority in the administration of all well-conducted States, and secondly, the payment of due and becoming regard to Indian authority in determining India's needs. I am making no vain boast when I say that in defending these principles as I have sought to do, and in sacrificing my position sooner than sacrifice them, I have behind me the whole of the civil services in India, the unanimous weight of non-official English opinion in this country, an overpowering preponderance of Indian opinion, and I will add, which is more significant still, the support of the greater part of the Indian Army. I have not one word to say in derogation of those who may hold opposite views ; but speaking for the last time as Viceroy of India I am entitled to say why in a few hours I shall cease to be Viceroy in India ; and I am also entitled to point out that in speaking for the last time as Viceroy of the country which I have administered for nearly seven years, I am speaking, as I believe no single one of my predecessors has ever been able to speak toa similar extent, with the whole of that country behind me. And, Gentlemen, you may depend upon it, the principles have not vanished, though they have momentarily disappeared. They will reappear, and that before very long.

It is a much pleasanter subject to turn from myself to the nobleman whose ship is hourly drawing nearer to these shores and who the day after to-morrow will take over the task that I lay down. It is a pleasure to me to be succeeded by a lifelong. friend. But it is a much greater pleasure to know that India will gain a Viceroy of ripe experience, of a strong sense of duty, of sound judgment, and of great personal charm. I hope that the rough seas through which I have sometimes ridden may leave smooth waters in which his keel may glide, and from the depth of my heart I wish him a tranquil and triumphant Viceroyalty.

And now, as the moment comes for me to utter the parting words, I am a little at a loss to know what they should be. A week ago, a man said to me, 'Do you really love India?' I could not imagine if he was jesting. 'Love India!' I replied, 'why otherwise I should have cut myself adrift from my own country for the best seven years of my life, why should I have given to this country the best of my poor health and strength, why should I have come back in the awful circumstances of a year ago, why should I have resigned my office sooner than see injury done to her now?' 'Good' he said, 'I was merely trying you—I knew it as well as every one else.'

Gentlemen, you all know it. There is not a man in this room, there is not an impartial man in India, there is not a Bengali patriot who now denounces me for giving him the boon for which he will one day bless my name, who does not know that no Englishman ever stepped on to the shores of India who had a more passionate devotion for the country than he who is now bidding it farewell. Nor will any Englishman ever have left it more resolved to the best of his humble abilities and strength, to continue to do justice in England to India—India who after two hundred years still stands like some beautiful stranger before her captors so defenceless, so forlorn, so little understood, so little known. She stands in need as much as ever—perhaps more than ever when such strange experiments are made by many whose knowledge of her does not extend beyond the fringe of her garment,—of being championed and spoken for and saved from insult or defamation. Perhaps my voice for India may not always be identical with that of all her sons, for some of them, as I have said, see or speak very differently from me. But it will be a voice raised on behalf not of a section or a fraction, but so far as the claim may be made, of all India. And in any case, it will be of an India whose development must continue to be a British duty, whose fair treatment is a test of British character, and whose destinies are bound up with those of the British race. So far as in me lies it will be a voice raised in the cause of impartial justice and fair dealing; and, most of all, seeing that Indian interests are not bartered away or sacrificed or selfishly pawned in the financial or economic adjustments of Empire.

A hundred times in India have I said to myself, Oh, that to every Englishman in this country, as he ends his work, might be truthfully applied the praise, "Thou hast loved righteousness and hated iniquity!"* No man has, I believe, ever served India faithfully of whom that could not be said. All other triumphs are tinsel and sham. Perhaps there are few of us who make anything but a poor approximation to that ideal. But let it be our ideal all the same. To fight for the right, to abhor the imperfect, the unjust or the mean, to swerve neither to the right hand nor to the left, to care nothing for flattery or applause or odium or abuse—it is so easy to have any of them in India—never to let your enthusiasm be soured or your courage grow dim, but to remember that the Almighty has placed your hand on the greatest of his ploughs, in whose furrow the nations of the future are germinating and taking shape, to drive the blade a little

---

These words are directly taken from the Epistle of St. Paul to the Hebrews: "Thou hast loved righteousness, and hated iniquity; therefore God, even thy God, hath anointed thee with the oil of gladness above thy fellows." (I. 9.). But of course they are an echo of the stirring words of the Psalmist: "Thou lovest righteousness, and hatest wickedness; therefore God, thy God, hath anointed thee with the oil of gladness above thy fellows." (XLV. 7.)

The Archbishop of Armagh has referred to this quotation in his poem welcoming Lord Curzen on his return home.

forward in your time, and to feel that somewhere among these millions you have left a little justice or happiness or prosperity, a sense of manliness or moral dignity, a spring of patriotism, a dawn of intellectual enlightenment, or a stirring of duty where it did not before exist—that is enough, that is the Englishman's justification in India. It is good enough for his watchword while he is here, for his epitaph when he is gone. I have worked for no other aim. Let India be my judge.

SPEECH AT THE UNITED SERVICE CLUB, SIMLA.

On September 30th, Lord Curzon attended the dinner given in his honour by the United Service Club at Simla. There was an unusual attendance. His Honour the Lieutenant Governor of the Panjab, Sir Charles Rivaz, was among those present. The Honourable Mr. Hewett, Member of the Viceroy's Council, presided, and in a happy little speech proposed his health. Whereupon Lord Curzon responded as follows :—

Mr. Hewett, Your Honour and Gentlemen :—I desire to thank the members of this Club for the distinguished compliment that they have paid to me in inviting me to be their guest at this dinner to-night and also for the large and, as I believe, unexampled numbers that have collected within this room to do me honour. I have listened with much gratitude though not without a good deal of compunction, to the kind remarks that have fallen from the lips of the chairman, the Hon. Mr. Hewett. I feel it is my good fortune that the task of proposing my health on this parting occasion should have fallen into his hands ; for in one capacity or another, Mr. Hewett has been one of my foremost colleagues during the last seven years. When I came out to India as Viceroy, he was Home Secretary, one of the most important posts in our administration. Then he became head of a Local Government proceeding to the Central Provinces, that well-known threshold to higher office. Finally, when it became necessary to appoint the new Member for Commerce and Industry he was the one Civilian pre-eminently well qualified for the post.

Thus he has seen many sides of the work of Government during recent years, and if he can speak, as he has done, of that which has been attempted, and in part accomplished, the compliment is all the greater because of the man who utters it. There was one remark in Mr. Hewett's speech by which I could not fail to be personally touched and that was the sentence in which he spoke of Lady Curzon as my comrade. It is true that in the arduous and, as he remarked, isolated position which the Viceroy of India is compelled to occupy, he is sustained by the solace of those who are nearest and dearest to him. In this way, my work has been lightened by the influences that have always been at my side. The part which India fills in the memory and affections of Lady Curzon is not inferior to that which she occupies in my own, and when we have left this country, my heart will not alone be left behind but a considerable portion of hers will be here also. Gentlemen, I do not stand here to-night to discuss controversial topics. They will work out to their appointed issue by processes which we cannot discern or, at any rate, cannot at present discern. History will write its verdict upon them with unerring pen and we need not to-night anticipate the sentence. I stand here rather as one who has laboured and wrought amongst you to the best of his ability through long and stirring years and who rises for the last time to address the comrades who have shared his toil, and, if he has anywhere conquered, have enabled him to conquer.

I cannot approach such a task without emotion and I cannot feel sure of being able to discharge it with credit. I have referred to the position of peculiar isolation in which the Viceroy stands, and I prefer rather, in what I have to say to-night, to turn my attention to those aspects of his work which bring him into contact with others. The relation of the Viceroy to the services in India is one of a peculiar and unexampled description. He is over them, but not of them; he is not attached to them, as a party politican in England is to his party, by the ties of long fellow-service in a common cause. His link with them is one of official rank, not of personal identity, and it is limited to a few years, at the most, instead of being spread over a lifetime. He is almost invariably from the nature of the case a stranger, brought out from England and placed for a short time in supreme charge. I always thought it a remarkable thing in these circumstances, and a proof of the loyalty and devotion to duty which is instinct in Englishmen, that the Indian Services should extend to the Viceroy the fidelity and the support which they do. In my own case, my feeling for the Indian Service was formed and was stated many years before I came to this country as Viceroy, and I cannot be suspected, therefore, of any after-thought, in declaring it now. When I brought out my book about Persia more than thirteen years ago, having written it, in the main, in the interests of Indian defence, I dedicated* it to the Civil and Military Services in India, and, there immediately after the title page, I spoke about them in language which represented my profound conviction then and represents it still. You may imagine, therefore, with what pride I found myself placed at the head of these Services seven years ago, and given the opportunity of co-operating for great ends with such strenuous and expert allies.

It will always, I think, remain the greatest recollection of my public life that for this, not inconsiderable, period, I was permitted to preside over the most efficient and the most high-minded public service which I believe to exist in the world. Gentlemen, our official generations in India move so quickly, particularly in the higher ranks, that a Viceroy who has been here seven years ends by finding himself the *doyen* of the official hierarchy, and feels that he is old almost before he has ceased to be young. Such has been my own experience, though the Viceroy has colleagues in his Cabinet or Council, lately revised, to the normal duration of five years.

I have served with no fewer than twenty Councillors in my time, and in the ten local Governments, I have well co-operated with nearly thirty Governors, Lieutenant-Governors and Chief

---

* See note at the end of this speech, p. 24

Commissioners. Perhaps, therefore, I may claim an exceptional right to speak. It does indeed seem to me a remarkable thing that work, pursued under the conditions of pressure which have characterised our recent activities, and with responsible agents so varied, so important, and so numerous, should have been carried on with so much smoothness and good feeling and, if I may speak for the treatment which I have personally received, with such generous consideration and personal regard. I venture to assert not as a boast or as a compliment, but as a fact, that there has never been a time when the relations between the Supreme Government and the Heads of the local Governments have been so free from friction or so harmonious. In the odd volumes of our proceedings, which it has been my duty to study at midnight hours, I have sometimes come across peppery letters or indignant remonstrances, and have seen the spectacle of infuriated Proconsuls strutting up and down the stage. We now live not in the iron or stone age, when implements of this description were, at any rate figuratively, in constant use, but in the age of milk and honey when we all sit down together to devour the grapes of Eshcol, by which I mean the surpluses that are provided for us by the Finance Department. Even that Department has ceased to be a nightmare to the good as well as a terror to the evil, and has assumed an urbanity in harmony with the spirit of the time.

No doubt, these results are partially due, as I have hinted, to the more prosperous circumstances through which we have been passing, and to the greater devolution of financial responsibility upon local Governments that we have carried out. But they also reflect a positive desire on our part to be everywhere on the best of terms with the local Governments and their heads, and to avoid nagging interference and petty overruling ; and they have everywhere been met by a loyalty and a friendly co-operation on their part, which I should like to take this opportunity to acknowledge, and which have made the relations between the Viceroy and the Governors and Lieutenant-Governors with whom he has served, one of the most agreeable episodes of my term of office.

I am not one of those who hold the view, that local Governments are hampered in their administration by excessive centralisation, or that any great measures of devolution would produce better results. In so far as there has been centralisation in the past, it has been in the main because, under the quinquennial contract system, the local Governments had not the means with which to extend themselves, and there cannot be much autonomy where there are not financial resources. Now that we have substituted permanent financial agreements for the terminable agreements, and have placed the local Governments in funds, they can proceed with internal development with as much freedom as can be desired. I am not in favour of removing altogether, or even of slackening the central control, for I believe that, with due allowance for the astonishing diversity of local conditions, it is essential that there should be certain uniform principles running through our entire administration, and nothing could be worse, either for India or for British Dominion in India, than that the country should be split up into a number of separate and rival units, very much like the Austro-Hungarian Empire in Europe, where the independent factors are only held together by the nexus of a single crown.

The various enquiries that have been conducted into Administration in my time, notably into education, famine, irrigation and police, have shown how easy it is for central principles to be forgotten, and for indifference at head-quarters to breed apathy and want of system lower down. I believe, therefore, in a strong Government of India gathering into its own hands and controlling all the reins; but I would ride the local Governments on the snaffle and not on the curb, and I would do all in our power to consult their feelings, to enhance their dignity, and to stimulate their sense of responsibility and power. The head of a local Administration in India, and I speak in the presence of one to-night, possesses great initiative and an authority which is scarcely understood out of India. Sometimes in the past, these prerogatives have been used to develop dissension, and the Supreme Government has,—so I am told,—scarcely been on speaking terms with some of its principal lieutenants. I have been lucky in escaping all such experiences, and every Governor, Lieutenant-Governor, or Chief Commissioner whom I have known, has exerted himself with equal loyalty to conform to the general policy rather than to pursue his own. This, however, is rather a digression into which I have wandered, and I must get back to my subject at the point at which I left it.

Even more than with the heads of local Governments, have I necessarily been brought into contact with my own colleagues in the Government of India. I speak primarily of the Members of Council and secondarily of the Secretaries to the Government of India, which is governed not by an individual but by a committee. No important step can be taken without the assent of a majority of that committee, which in practice cuts both ways. It is the tendency in India, as elsewhere, but much more in India than anywhere else that I have known, to identify the acts of Government with the head of the administration. The Viceroy is constantly spoken of as though he, and he alone, were the Government. This, of course, is unjust to his colleagues who are equally responsible with himself, and very often deserve the credit which he unfairly obtains. On the other hand, it is sometimes unfair to him, for he may have to bear the entire responsibility for administrative acts or policies, which were participated in and perhaps originated by them. In these rather difficult circumstances, which perhaps work out on the whole in a fair equation, it is a consolation to me to reflect—and this is the only Cabinet secret that I am going to divulge,—that during my seven years of office, there has not been a single important question whether of internal or external politics, in which the Government of India have not been absolutely unanimous, unless you except the last of all where the unanimity was scarcely broken.

I believe this to be unexampled in the history of Indian

administration. In the previous records of Indian Government, I have often come across sparring matches between the illustrious combatants, and contentious minutes used to be fired off like grape-shot at the head of the Secretary of State. I can only recall three occasions on which a minute dissenting from the decision of the majority of the Council has been sent home in the whole of my time, and I venture to think that with a Council, representing so many different interests and points of view, this indicates a very remarkable and gratifying unity. Certainly, it has not been purchased by any sacrifice of independent judgment. The Viceroy has no more weight in his Council than any individual member of it. What it does show is, that the Government of India, in approaching the work of reconstruction and reform with which we have charged ourselves, has been inspired by a single spirit and has pursued a common aim. I recall with pride that in every considerable undertaking we have been an absolutely united body, united not merely in identity of opinion but in a common enthusiasm, and on this parting occasion it may be permissible for me to say, both of the distinguished Civilians and the eminent soldiers with whom it has been my privilege to serve, that I thank them with a gratitude, which it would be impossible to exaggerate, for a co-operation that has converted the years of toil into years of honourable pleasure, that will always remain one of the happiest recollections of my life.

Then I turn to the Secretaries to Government, those faithful and monumental workers, who dig in the mounds of the past and excavate the window of our ancestors, who prepare our cases for us and write our official letters and despatches, and generally keep us all from going wrong. I have served with many Secretaries to Government in my time, and I do not believe that in any administration in the world is the standard of trained intelligence or devotion to duty, in the service which they represent, so uniformly high. My consolation in thinking of them is that a better reward than my poor thanks lies before them. As they gradually blossom into Chief Commissioners and Lieutenant-Governors and Members of Council, they will earn the fuller recognition to which they are entitled, and in my retirement, I shall for years to come, have the pleasure of seeing the higher posts of Indian Administration filled by men, with whom I have been privileged to work, and of whose capacity for the most responsible offices I have had such abundant opportunity to convince myself. Some paper at home said the other day that I had not founded a school. There was no need to do that, for it was here already. But I have assisted to train one, and if the tests have sometimes been rather exacting, I may perhaps say in self-defence, that I have never imposed upon others a burden which I was not willing to accept myself.

What I have said of Members and Secretaries is not less true of the officers who have served under them in the Departments of Government. When I came to Simla I observed that I regarded this place as the workshop of the Administration, and such indeed during the last few years I believe it has truly been.

It was Burke who remarked in one of his speeches that there is one sight that is never seen in India, and that is the grey head of an Englishman. As I look about me, I begin to think that we must live in a rather different and degenerate age, and I am not sure that a certain guilty consciousness does not steal over my mind. I must confess that I have heard it whispered that Simla has acquired in recent times an unenviable reputation for staidness and sobriety, and I believe that invidious epithets have even been applied to the hospitable and once light-hearted institution in which I am now privileged to be entertained. Gentlemen, must I offer an apology for this alleged falling-off from the standards of the past? No, I do nothing of the sort; I do not allow for a moment that we have pursued duty at the cost of the amenities of life. I most certainly have not done so. We have all had our hours of gaiety and ease at Simla, and very pleasant they have been; but we have certainly set work before play, we have spent more time in school than out of it, and for my own part I believe that an incalculable benefit has been conferred upon the entire Service by the example of those public servants who used to be accused of idling away their time on the hills, but who now make up for the refreshing altitude in which they labour by the arduous and unremitting character of the labour itself.

We have finally killed the fallacy, perhaps never true at all, and certainly least of all, true now, that the summer capital of Government is a place where it is all summer and not much government; and if a Royal Commission were sent round to investigate the Factories of the Empire, I should await with perfect equanimity the place that Simla would occupy in its report. Gentlemen, there is one error against which I think that we ought very particularly to be on our guard. I should not like any of us, because we happen to be at the head-quarters of Government, to delude ourselves into thinking that we are the only people or even the principal people who run the Indian machine. It would be quite untrue. India may be governed from Simla or Calcutta, but it is administered from the plains. We may issue the orders and correct the mistakes, but the rank and file of the army are elsewhere; and if we make the plans of battles they fight them. Let me not forfeit this opportunity of expressing my feelings towards the entire Civil Service of India for the loyal co-operation that I have received from them. At the beginning I believe, they thought me rather a disturbing element in the economy of Indian official existence; but when they saw that my interests were theirs, and theirs mine, because there is no one who so much benefitted by increased efficiency in administration as the administrator himself, they gave me every assistance in their power, and no one is more sincerely conscious than myself, that if success has anywhere been obtained it has not been in the Secretariat alone, but in the District office, in the court, and, I would even add, in the fields.

Gentlemen, what is the secret of success in the Indian Services, Civil and Military alike? It lies not in systems or rules, not even exclusively in training or education. It consists in the man. If revenue assessments are to be fair and equitable to the people, it will not be because of the resolutions which the Government of India have issued to regulate them, but because a sympathetic settlement-officer has been sent to carry them out. If one Division or District is discontented and another tranquil, it will usually be because one has the wrong man at the head and the other the right one; if one young chief degenerates into extravagance or dissipation, while another develops into a statesman and a ruler of men, it will probably be found that the former has a weak political officer or an incompetent tutor, while the other has been in strong and capable hands; if one regiment is efficient while another is soft or has a bad record, look to the commanding officer and you will commonly find the clue. Therefore, I say, in India, as elsewhere, but most of all in India, give me the man, the best that England can produce, the best that India can train. To every head of an Indian Administration, to every chief of an office, I would say, pick out the best men, run them to the front, give them their chance—that is the whole secret of administration. I have said a hundred times, and I say it again, that there is no service in the world where ability, and character quite as much as ability, are more sure of their reward than the Indian Service. Nothing can keep them down, for they are the pivot and fulcrum of our rule. So long as we can continue to send to this country the pick of the youth of our own, so long as they are inspired by high standards of life and conduct, so long as each officer, Civil or Military, regards himself in his own sphere as the local custodian of British honour and the local representative of the British name, so long we are safe and India is safe also. For the good man makes other men good, the efficient officer spreads efficiency about him, and the sympathetic officer diffuses an atmosphere of loyalty and contentment.

Gentlemen, perhaps I may be allowed to interpolate a word in this place, about the particular branch of the Service of which I have been more especially the head: I allude to the Political Department. The Viceroy, as taking the Foreign Office under his personal charge, has a greater responsibility for the officers of that Department than of any other. A good Political is a type of officer difficult to train, indeed training by itself will never produce him, for there are required in addition qualities of tact and flexibility, of fibre and gentlemanly bearing, which are an instinct rather than an acquisition. The public at large hardly realises what the Political may be called upon to do. At one time he may be grinding at the Foreign Office, at another he may be required to stiffen the administration of a backward Native State, at a third he may be presiding over a Jirga of unruly tribes on the frontier, at a fourth he may be defining a boundary amid the wilds of Tibet or the sands of Seistan. There is no more varied or responsible service in the world than the Political Department of the Government of India; and right well have I been served in it from the mature and experienced officer who handles a Native Chief with velvet glove, to the young Military Political who packs up his trunk at a moment's notice and goes off to Arabia or Kurdistan.

I commend the Political Department of the Government of India to all who like to know the splendid and varied work of which Englishmen are capable, and I hope that the time may never arise when it will cease to draw to itself the abilities and the finest characters that the Services in India can produce.

Gentlemen, I have been speaking so far of the agents with whom I have been permitted to work. Let me add, if I may, a few words about the work itself. If I were asked to sum it up in a single word, I would say: Efficiency. That has been our gospel, the key-note of our administration. I remember once reading in a native newspaper, which was attacking me very bitterly, the sentence: "As for Lord Curzon he cares for nothing but efficiency." Exactly, Gentlemen; but I hardly think that when I am gone this is an epitaph of which I need feel greatly ashamed. There were three respects, in which a short experience taught me, that a higher level of efficiency under our administration was demanded. The first was in the despatch of business. Our methods were very dignified, our procedure very elaborate and highly organised, but the pace was apt to be the reverse of speedy. I remember in my first year settling a case, that had been pursuing the even tenour of its way, without, as far as I could ascertain, exciting the surprise or ruffling the temper of an individual for sixty-one years. I drove my pen like a stiletto into its bosom, I buried it with exultation and I almost danced upon its grave. Gentlemen, I really think that not merely the new rules that we have adopted, but the new principles that are at work, have done a good deal to assist the despatch of business, and I hope that there may not be any backsliding or relapse in the future. It was one of Sir John Lawrence's sayings, that procrastination is the thief of efficiency as well as of time, and though I would not say that an administration is good in proportion to its pace, I would certainly say that it cannot be good if it is habitually and needlessly slow. Our second object was the overhauling of our existing machinery, which had got rusty and had run down. There is scarcely a department of the Government, or a branch of the Service, which we have not, during the last few years, explored from top to bottom, improving the conditions of service where they were obsolete or inadequate, formulating a definite programme of policy or action, and endeavouring to raise the standard and the tone. And, thirdly, we had to provide new machinery to enable India to grapple with new needs.

Perhaps, there is nothing which the public has shown so general an inability to understand, as the fact that a new world of industry and enterprise, and social and economic advance is dawning upon India. New continents and islands leap above the horizon as they did before the navigators of the Elizabethan Age; but if I am right, if agriculture and irrigation and commerce and industry have great and unknown futures before them, then the Government which in this country is nearly everything, must be ready with appliances to enable it to shape and to direct these new forms of extension. You cannot administer India according to modern standards but on the old lines. Some people talk as though, when we create new departments and posts, we are merely adding to the burden of Government. No, we are doing nothing of the sort. The burden of Government is being added to by tendencies and forces outside of ourselves, which we are powerless to resist, but not powerless to control. We are merely providing the mechanism to cope with it. Of course we must not be blind to the consideration that progress is not a mere matter of machinery alone, and that life and the organisation of life are very different things. There is always danger of converting an efficient staff into a bureaucracy, and, while perfecting the instruments, of ignoring the free play of natural forces. Against that tendency I would implore all those who are engaged in work in India, to be peculiarly on their guard, for it may be said of reforms everywhere, and here perhaps most of all, that what is contrary to nature is doomed to perish, and that what is organic will alone survive.

Gentlemen, I am afraid that I am becoming too philosophic for the dinner table, and I will revert to the concrete. Of the actual schemes that we have undertaken, with the objects that I have attempted to describe, I will say nothing here. You know them as well as I do; you are the joint authors of many of them, and time alone will show whether they have been the offspring of a premature and feverish energy, or whether they have taken root and will endure. I desire no other or fairer test. In some cases it is already in operation, sifting the good from the bad, and giving glimpses of the possible verdict of the future. I will only take one instance, because it is familiar to you all and because there may be officers here present who were orginally doubtful about the wisdom or propriety of the change. I speak of the creation of the North-West Frontier Province, which was carved out of the Punjab more than four years ago. You will all remember the outcries of the prophets of evil : it was going to inflict an irreparable wound upon the prestige of the Punjab Government, it was to overwhelm the Foreign Department with tiresome work, it was to encourage ambitious officers to gasconade upon the frontier; it was the symbol of a forward and "jingo" policy and would speedily plunge us into another campaign. We do not hear so much of these prophecies now, and I venture to assert that there is not an officer here present, from the Lieutenant-Governor of the Punjab downwards, who would go back upon the decision of 1901. It has given peace and contentment upon the border, and has substituted the prompt despatch of frontier cases for endless perambulations and delays.

But the creation of the Frontier Province did not stand by itself. It was merely one symptom of a frontier policy which we have been pursuing quietly but firmly for seven years. I will utter no prophecy to-night and will indulge in no boast. I am content with the simple facts, that for seven years we have not had a single frontier expedition,—the only seven years of which this can be said since the frontier passed into British hands,— and that whereas in the five years, from 1894 to 1899, the Indian tax-payer had to find four-and-a-half million pounds sterling for frontier warfare, the total cost of military operations on the entire North-

West Frontier in the last seven years has only been £248,000, and that was for the semi-pacific operation of the Mahsud blockade.

And now, gentlemen, I must not detain you further. This is one of the last speeches that I shall be called upon to make in India, and I have made it, through you who are present here to-night, to the Services which I have captained and which I have been privileged to lead. We have worked together in good report and in evil report. India is in some respects a hard task-master. She takes her toll of health and spirits and endurance and strength. A man's love for the country is apt sometimes to be soured by calumny, his passion for work to be checked by the many obstacles to be encountered, his conception of duty to be chilled by disappointment or delay. Such have sometimes been my own feelings, such I daresay have often been the feelings of those whom I am addressing; but this is only an ephemeral depression. When it comes upon us let us cast it off, for it is not the real sentiment of the Indian Service. As the time comes for us to go, we obtain a clearer perspective. It is like a sunset in the hills after the rains: the valleys are wrapped in sombre shadow, but the hill-tops stand out sharp and clear. Our Indian career, be it long as it has been or will be in the case of many who are here to-night, or relatively short as in mine, we feel that we can never have such a life again, so crowded with opportunity, so instinct with duty, so touched with romance. We forget the rebuffs and the mortification, we are indifferent to the slander and the pain. Perhaps if we forget these, others will equally forget our shortcomings and mistakes. We remember only the noble cause for which we have worked together, the principles of equity and justice and righteousness for which we have contended, and the good, be it ever so little, that we have done,—and India becomes the lodestar of our memories as she has hitherto been of our duty. For us she can never again be "the Land of Regrets."

NOTE.—The Dedication of Lord Curzon's book on Persia, 1892, referred to by His Lordship on p. 16, is as follows:

TO

THE OFFICIALS, CIVIL AND MILITARY, IN INDIA

WHOSE HANDS UPHOLD

THE NOBLEST FABRIC YET REARED

BY THE GENIUS OF A CONQUERING NATION

I DEDICATE THIS WORK

THE UNWORTHY TRIBUTE OF THE PEN TO A CAUSE

WHICH BY JUSTICE OR WITH THE SWORD

IT IS THEIR HIGH MISSION TO DEFEND

BUT WHOSE ULTIMATE SAFEGUARD IS THE SPIRIT

OF THE BRITISH PEOPLE

SPEECH BEFORE THE SECRETARIAT CLERKS AT SIMLA.

On October 13th, Lord Curzon received an Address from the subordinate officials of the Secretariat at Simla, to which he replied in the following words, which made a deep impression on those assembled and were most enthusiastically received by them:—

Gentlemen,—Among the many hundreds of expressions of compliment and regard that have reached me from all classes of the community during the past few weeks, there is not one to which I attach a higher value than the tribute which is now offered to me by yourselves, as the representatives of the ministerial establishments of Government or what are often generically described as the European and Native clerks. The tribute is the more affecting and valuable in my eyes because, as you tell me in your address, it is unprecedented in the annals of your service, and because I have the best of reasons for knowing that it springs spontaneously from the hearts of those who tender it. Every man who vacates an office, however great, in which he has been placed above his fellow-creatures, likes to think that if regret is anywhere felt at his departure, it is not confined to those in high place or station alone, but is shared by the much larger number to whom fortune has assigned a lowlier, though not necessarily a less responsible position in his surroundings.

Gentlemen, ever since I came to India, my heart has been drawn towards the subordinate officers of Government. In the first place, it seemed to me that they were a most industrious and painstaking body of men, labouring for long hours at a task which, though it tends to become mechanical, is very far from being lifeless, but demands qualities of diligence and accuracy and honesty of no mean order. I have often remarked that the best Indian clerk is, in my opinion, the best clerk in the world, for he is very faithful to detail and very unsparing of himself. Secondly, I observed that many members of the class to which I am referring are obliged to serve the Government at a distance from their homes, sometimes in places that are uncongenial and expensive, and that their work is apt to be pursued amid rather monotonous and depressing surroundings.

And thirdly, I found, after a little experience, not merely that these classes were rather forlorn and friendless, but that there was a tendency when they made mistakes or were guilty of offences to be somewhat hard upon them, and on occasions to hustle them out of employment on pension upon hasty and inadequate grounds. I set myself, therefore, to try to understand the position and, if possible, to alleviate the lot of the classes of whom I have been speaking, and the new rules which we have passed or systems that we have introduced about the abolition of fining in the Departments of Government, the observance of public holidays, the leave rules of the subordinate services, the rank and pay of the higher grades among them, and the allowances and pensionary prospects of all classes, have, I hope, done a good deal to mitigate some of the hardships that had been felt, and to place them in a more assured and comfortable position in the future. It was on similar grounds that I pressed for the appointment of the Committee to deal with Simla allowances, and although I do not know if it will be possible for me to pass final orders upon the subject before I go, yet the main thing is that the question has been seriously investigated and cannot now be dropped. Personally, I have taken, if possible, an even warmer interest in the opportunities that have presented themselves to me of investigating memorials and grievances, and now and then of rescuing individuals from excessive punishment or undeserved disgrace.

You know, Gentlemen, for I have often stated it in public, the feelings that I hold about the standards of British rule in this country. We are here before everything else to give justice, and a single act of injustice is in my view a greater stain upon our rule than much larger errors of policy or judgment. I have sometimes thought that in dealing with subordinates, and particularly native subordinates, there is a tendency to be rather peremptory in our methods, and to visit transgression or suspected transgression with the maximum of severity for flagrant misconduct, whether among the high or low, European or native. I have never felt a ray of sympathy, but I have always thought that a small man, whose whole fortune and livelihood were at stake, deserved just as much consideration for his case, if not more so, than a big man, and that we ought to be very slow to inflict a sentence of ruin unless the proof were very strong. The most striking case, in the history of the world, of mercy in high places, is that of Abraham Lincoln, the President of the United States, who was assassinated. He was sometimes condemned for it at the time, but it is one of his glories in history. A Viceroy of India has no such opportunities as occur to the head of a great Government at a time of civil war. Yet as the final court of appeal on every case, great or small, amid the vast population of India, he has chances that occur to but few. I think that he ought to take them. I have tried to do so. I can recall long night-hours, spent in the effort to unravel some tangled case of alleged misconduct resulting in the dismissal of a poor unknown native subordinate. Perhaps those hours have not been the worst spent of my time in India, and the simple letters of gratitude from the score or more of humble individuals, whom I have thus saved from ruin, have been equally precious in my eyes with the resolutions of public bodies or the compliments of princes.

Gentlemen, you may be sure that in bidding you farewell I don't forget the faithful though silent services that you have rendered to me. Far down below at the bottom of the pit you have striven and toiled, sending up to the surface the proceeds of your labour, which others then manipulate and convert to the public use. I hope that the Government will always be considerate to you and mindful of your services. For my own part, it will remain one of my pleasantest recollections, that I was able during my time in India to show you some practical sympathy, and that you came forward of your own accord at the end to testify your recognition.

SPEECH TO THE SIMLA MUNICIPALITY.

On October 17th, Lord Curzon was presented with an Address by the Municipality of Simla, on which occasion His Excellency took his farewell of the Summer Capital in the following speech :—

Gentlemen,—It is just six and a half years ago since I drove up to Simla by the tonga road and was received by the President and members of the then Municipality upon my arrival at Vice-regal Lodge. In a few days' time Lady Curzon and I will be driving down for the last time by the same road. Not that we are indifferent to the advantages of the railway, of which I have on several occasions availed myself, but as we came, so we like to go, preferring that Simla should remain in our memories as a place, a little detached from the bustle and hurry of modern life, which sweeps us all into its vortex as it rushes along. When I came here, I rather ignorantly defended the summer migration of Government to Simla. I say ignorantly, because I do not now think that the movement required defence. Certainly the railway has taken away the last valid argument of aloofness, and anyone who is aware of the enormous rise in the population of this place in recent years, cannot rightly accuse it of being any longer inaccessible to the outer world. The danger is entirely in the opposite direction, namely, that the rush of people to Simla will one day be too great and will be in excess of the capacities of the place either as regards accommodation or health. It is to these large questions of development that those who are responsible for the administration of Simla, both now and in the future, must turn their attention.

A hill-station that requires in the summer to provide a habitation for 4,000 Europeans and 39,000 natives on the slender edges of a number of hills, that were certainly not intended by nature for any such purpose, necessarily suggests very difficult problems of housing, sanitation, water supply and lighting. These problems are in my judgment only in their initial stages, and they will need the application of very wide views and the introduction of corresponding changes, before they are satisfactorily solved. I have often pictured to myself the Simla of the future with its suburbs spread out over the surrounding hills instead of huddled together on the central summits, connected with its outskirts by some mechanical means of traction, combining the amenities of town and country, and administered on bold statesmanlike lines. These schemes will be realised, if ever they are realised, at a later date. In the meantime the Government of India during my time has done what lay in its power to promote expansion on intelligent principles, by the very large grant of twenty lakhs that we made last year to the local Government from Imperial funds, to extend your boundaries and improve your communications, and by insistence whenever possible upon the anticipation of future requirements not less than upon the satisfaction of existing needs.

For my own part, I can truly say that I have taken the keenest personal interest in the external appearance of the buildings of Simla, and with the artistic assistance of that very talented architect, Sir Swinton Jacob, I have succeeded in bequeathing to Simla what I unhesitatingly describe as the finest public building at a hill station in India. I allude to the new Secretariat on Gorton Hill, which may appropriately be contrasted with the painted card-board structures, which the taste of an earlier generation thought an adequate setting for the labours of the military authorities. Our new building would not do discredit to the castle-crowned Highlands of Bavaria or to the banks of the Rhine. I also did my best in conjunction with the Bishop of Lahore, a few years ago, to provide Simla with a new Church more befitting the needs and dignity of the Capital of Government ; but the forces against us were too strong and we even encountered some persons who thought the existing fabric beautiful. There is one public work that I bitterly regret never having had the opportunity of taking in hand, and that is a new Town Hall. When the earthquake took place this year, I looked fondly to its powerful co-operation to provide me with a legitimate excuse by levelling the structure in which I am now speaking to the ground ; but the earthquake failed lamentably at the critical moment, and the last sight of Simla that I shall catch from the tonga road as I turn the final corner, will be the first that arrested my eye as I came up six years ago, namely the gaunt and graceless protuberance against the sky line within whose walls I have enjoyed so much pleasure, and where I am now receiving at your hands this final compliment, but whose external appearance is so unworthy both of the character of the station and of the purposes to which it is applied. Another considerable building that has been erected in my time has been the Walker Hospital. I wish that we had constructed an edifice more in harmony with the liberality of the donor. That hospital renders great service, but in a better locality and with finer buildings might, I think, render even greater.

During our stay in Simla, Lady Curzon and I have invariably been treated with the greatest courtesy and kindness by every class of the community. We have endeavoured to the best of our ability to identify ourselves with your interests, and wherever we go or whatever becomes of us, there are features and incidents in Simla life that can never be obliterated from our minds. The familiar drive round Jakko, the still more beautiful ride round Summer Hills, the sudden bursting of green on the hills after the first week of the rains, the undulating downs of Naldera and the full moon riding at midnight above the deodar spires, the September sunsets over the weltering plains, and finally the first reappearance of the long lost snows in October coming simultaneously with the crisp exultation of the autumn air,—all of these are scenes or sensations that are a part of our life for ever. With them, just as much as with the toil and moil of administrative work and official routine, Simla will be associated in our memory. Associated, too, will it always be with acts of kindness received from great and small, European and native, and with the hundreds of happinesses that compose the serenity of domestic life. These are the things that we shall always remember, and that are aptly summed up on this parting occasion in the graceful and a sympathetic language, with which you have attended here this morning to bid us farewell.

Gentlemen, I thank you most sincerely on Lady Curzon's behalf, and on my own, for the compliment which is an official echo of the spontaneous reception, accorded to us a week ago, by the townspeople, as we drove to the parting entertainment given to us in this building. Both of these tributes have touched us greatly.

SPEECH AT LAHORE.

On October 27th, Lord Curzon, on his arrival at Lahore,—the capital of the Punjab, so much favoured by Jahangir the Great Mughal, and afterwards the chief seat of the power of Ranjit Singh, the Sikh Lion of the Punjab,—received the Address from its Municipality to which he replied as follows :—

Gentlemen,—I greatly appreciate the compliment, that you have bestowed upon me, in addressing me for a second time on the eve of my departure from India. It is pleasant to learn from your own lips that my term of office has coincided with a period of uninterrupted progress both for this city, and for the whole province of the Punjab. I believe that a better service was never wrought to the province than when the tantalising and anxious burden of the Frontier management was taken from its shoulders, and it was left to pursue its own agricultural and commercial and industrial development on progressive and unhampered lines. The growth in prosperity and population, that has followed in the main from the construction of new canals and the colonisation of the reclaimed areas, has no parallel in the history of modern India. Not even plague, which has smitten you with so heavy a hand, has managed to retard this advance, and it must be a source of gratification to your Lieutenant-Governor, Sir C. Rivaz, to find that his devotion to the province, and his sympathetic rule of it, have been rewarded by such remarkable symptoms of progress.

The two great things in the Punjab are, in my view, to maintain the old class of yeomen immemorially connected with the soil, and to keep alive that sturdy and martial spirit that has given us the pick of our armed forces. I should think badly of any legislation or any administrative or political changes, that tend to sap either of these sources of vitality and thereby to lower the reputation of the Punjab before the world. I believe that the Land Alienation Bill, which I assisted to pass in the early part of my administration, has already done a good deal, and will do more, to keep upon the soil the hereditary owners. As for the army, I trust that increasing wealth and the higher standards of modern life will not in any degree diminish the military spirit of the races who dwell in these parts of India, or stop the flow of recruits to the Indian army. That army is required not merely to preserve internal order and to guard our frontiers, but also as a field of honourable employment for the masculine element in the population. It would be the greatest misfortune to India, if they became effeminate or if they were to desist from the hereditary and manly pursuit of arms.

Lately the province has suffered from another calamity, which has sufficed to show how well its citizens, official and private, could rise to the level of a great emergency, and also how much common feeling exists everywhere throughout the Indian continent. I speak of the earthquake in Kangra. In the early days, when the subscriptions seemed to be coming in rather slowly, I was afraid that we might not obtain the sums we required. But the most sanguine estimates, both of the Lieutenant-Governor and the Executive Committee and myself, were finally exceeded, and I calculate that the total sums, contributed both in this country and in England to the Civil and Military funds, must have amounted to over £110,000, which is, I think, both a very handsome and a very creditable total. The Government has helped the generosity of private donors, and so far as official and non-official patriotism in combination could avail to repair the disaster, this has certainly been done.

Gentlemen, I am glad to hear from you so good a record of Municipal progress in Lahore. Municipal training is the best form of education for public responsibilities, and Municipal administration, though not the most showy, is perhaps the most useful of the forms of government admitted in our constitution. I always rejoice to hear of native gentlemen throwing themselves with energy into the service of their fellow citizens, for, although for scientific and sanitary knowledge the training of the European expert is frequeutly necessary, it is the inhabitants of the country who ought to be most thoroughly cognizant of the needs and desires of their countrymen. You speak of the harmony with which your own Municipal institutions are worked, and from this I conclude that both of these classes co-operate heartily for the common good.

Lady Curzon is very grateful to you for the paragraph in your address, which you have devoted to her labours on behalf of her own sex in India. She has realised throughout that an Englishwoman in this country, and particularly one in high official station, has a duty towards her fellow-women just as definite as a male official has towards his fellow-men. That duty is to leave them if possible a little better than she found them. And no higher reward could she have than the feeling that both the institution which she inherited from one of her predecessors, Lady Dufferin, and that which she initiated herself, in memory of the late Queen Victoria, for the provision of Indian midwives, have done something to alleviate the sufferings or add to the comforts of Indian women. It only remains for us both to express our thanks to the members of the Municipal Committee for their combined welcome and good-bye to us this morning, and for me to say that this city, which I have four times visited as Viceroy, has always held, and will continue to hold a firm place in my affections, as the fit capital of not the least splendid and vigorous among the provinces of the Indian Empire.

SPEECH AT AGRA.

On October 11th, Lord Curzon arrived at Agra, the city of the Taj Mahal, and was presented with an Address by the Municipality, to which he replied in the following words :—

Gentlemen,—It is very good of you to address me a second time, and a reference to what passed between us on the previous occasion just six years ago, is of interest as marking the distance that has been travelled by both of us since December 1899. You have given to me this afternoon a record of your Municipal progress in the interval. The central position of Agra and its greatly improved railway connections are a source of no small advantage which all your competitors do not equally enjoy. Successive Lieutenant-Governors, and notably in recent years Sir Antony MacDonnell and Sir James La Touche, have devoted the closest personal attention to the city and its buildings. You can never fail to attract visitors, and in my judgment are certain to attract them in rapidly increasing numbers. With a Municipality, therefore, that is devoted, as yours appears to be, to the conscientious pursuit of its duties, which consists in making life here as healthy as possible for your residents and citizens, and with a reasonable immunity from the scourges of plague and famine by which you are liable to be, and have been, seriously afflicted, Agra is as certain as any place in India of a future of steadily advancing prosperity. It is a proud trust therefore that you have in your hands, and it must have been rendered all the easier and more agreeable to you, by the fact that Agra is one of those places which from its exquisite beauty and its many physical advantages cannot fail to excite, in a peculiar degree, the love and the local patriotism of its inhabitants.

You will shortly have the honour of welcoming here Their Royal Highnesses the Prince and Princess of Wales, and I have confidently assured them that there is no place in India where their stay will be more pleasant or which will leave a more abiding impression upon their memories. My own connection with Agra has, as you know, been mainly archæological during the past six years. I think that in my numerous visits here, and in the labours of renovation and repair that we have undertaken, I have learned to love this place more than any other spot in India. Here it is always peaceful and always beautiful, though sometimes, I must admit, a little warm ; and with each successive visit I have felt the sense of something accomplished and of visible progress made. This has been due to the enthusiasm with which the Lieutenant-Governors, the local officials, the Public Works Engineers and the Director-General of Aachæology, Mr. Marshall, and his subordinates, have all thrown themselves into the task. To every one of them it has, I am convinced, been a labour of love, and all of us have felt that we were not merely atoning for the errors of our predecessors, but leaving something that will recover or increase the fascination of Agra for those who come after us.

It is just eighteen years since I first drove up to the Taj through dusty lanes and a miserable bazaar, since I first was conducted over the Fort, where the Jahangir Mahal and exquisite buildings anterior to the time of Shah Jahan were either in the occupation of the military or were not shown to visitors at all, and since I visited Sikandra, then a deserted wilderness, and Fatehpur Sikri, glorious in its beauty but crumbling to decay. As I visit all those places again, and note their renovated condition, their orderly approaches, and the spirit of reverence with which they are now preserved, I cannot help feeling that the work is one of which we may feel proud. There is this also to be said about the work of archæological restoration throughout India, that it is one in which European and Indian can, and do, equally join. There is nothing to which the inhabitants of this country are more attached than their antiquities, there is nothing by which they were more distressed than their desecration and decay, and few things, I am convinced, have done more to bring the two people together, than the consciousness that the English are devoting themselves with sincerity and ardour to the restoration of the monuments of a race and a religion which are not their own, but for which they feel the most profound respect and veneration. No co-operation of this description is to be despised, for it has a value greatly in excess of its immediate or concrete results.

Gentlemen, Lady Curzon and I rejoice to be spending our last days in India in your midst, and we are grateful to you for joining in a farewell by the cordiality and unanimity of which we have been greatly impressed.

SPEECH TO THE DELHI MUNICIPALITY.

Lord Curzon being unable to visit Delhi—the historic City so memorably connected with his Viceroyalty by the great Imperial assemblage held there at the commencement of 1903, in honour of the Coronation of our King Emperor, and the old Capital of the Great Moghuls as well as of the old Hindu Kings—owing to indisposition, the Municipality of that City sent a Deputation to Agra, where he was then staying, to present its Address. After the presentation of the address on November 13th, Lord Curzon spoke as follows in reply :—

Gentlemen,—I am exceedingly sorry that I was not able to receive you at Delhi itself, where I had looked forward to spending three half days, when my recent illness came on, and where there was some important work that I desired to complete. It is very good of you to have travelled down here to present me with your address in person and I gratefully accept it at your hands. When I paid my first official visit to Delhi as Viceroy six years ago, I remember congratulating the members of the Delhi Municipality upon the model character of the address which they did me the honour of presenting. Then my work in India lay before me and both the Municipality and I could only speak in the future tense. Now it is finished and I cannot but feel a sense of pride that from the representatives of an ancient city that was the capital of an Empire and the possessor of an undying renown, I should have been thought worthy of such a tribute as that which you have just rendered.

Your remarks have related principally to archæology and to the many occasions on which I have been drawn to Delhi during the past six years in connection with antiquarian or other work. You are right in saying that I have taken a great interest in the place, because of its Imperial traditions and the beauty of its remains. You have particularly alluded to the restorations and repairs that have been undertaken in the shrines and tombs outside the City, principally those of Humayun, Safdar Jung, Isa Khan and Nizamuddin. I like to think that these famous men of the past still have their last resting places properly tended, and further, that the buildings so noble and the surroundings so gracious and fair are not allowed to fall into decay by the apathy or slovenliness of later generations. In the Fort a great deal more remains to be done. A considerable portion of the garrison is to be moved outside the city, and I hope we shall thus gradually get rid of those monstrous barracks which are now such an eyesore and offence. We are at present engaged in restoring the palace-gardens of the Moghul Emperors, of which the pavilions and water-courses still exist or can be reproduced.

I have, as you know, brought out a Florentine artificer in mosaics to replace the marble incrustations at the back of the throne, and I hope that a few years hence the interior of the Fort may present some slight resemblance—it cannot, I fear, be more, for so much has perished irretrievably—to what it was, not in the later days of the Moghuls when the moribund condition of the Empire was typified in the squalor and decay of the court, but in the resplendent times of Shah Jehan and Aurangzib. When the interior of the Fort has been renovated, I have always hoped that the artificial glacis outside, which was thrown up for defensive purposes after the Mutiny, may be removed, and that the magnificent red walls may then be seen to their base as they were up till fifty years ago.

You have alluded to the great pageant of the Coronation Durbar that was held at Delhi nearly three years ago. We are now engaged in commemorating with the assistance of Sir Aston Webb, one of the foremost of English architects, the common site of the two Durbars of 1877 and 1903 ; and when these works, which will combine architectural features with landscape gardening, have been completed, Delhi will possess a twentieth-century monument that will, I hope, compare favourably in beauty and impressiveness with the relics of earlier ages. I often see in unfriendly papers and speeches, a repetition of the old calumny that our Durbar in 1903 was a costly extravagance. The people who said it was going to cost two crores, became so enamoured of the phrase, that they have gone on ever since declaring that it *did* cost two crores, and one would almost imagine that some of them believe it, although the actual figures require to be multiplied no fewer than seven times in order to sustain the illusion You who are on the spot are cognizant of the facts, and the view which you entertain is that which will permanently commend itself to the judgment of history, namely, that the Durbar was a just and befitting celebration of the great event which it was intended to commemorate.

I will not now dwell upon the generous terms in which you have spoken of the general character of my administration, but will merely thank you for the unsolicited compliment you have concluded by expressing both a hope and a conviction that my affection for India will some time bring me out again. Who knows but that it may be perhaps as a simple tourist I may one day wander in a ticca gharry among the buildings and monuments that I loved, and to which, while responsible for them, I endeavoured to devote so true and reverent a care. However that may be, I can never forget my seven happy visits to Delhi as Viceroy or the courtesy and consideration which I have on so many occasions received from its inhabitants.

SPEECH AT JAMMU ON THE INSTALLATION OF H. H. THE MAHARAJAH OF KASHMIR.

On October 26th Lord Curzon arrived at Jammu, in Kashmir, specially to perform an unique ceremony, that of investing the young Maharajah of Kashmir with enhanced powers of administration as a Ruling Chief. This was the first time, as His Excellency pointed out, in the history of the Foreign Office, that this was done to a Native Prince. In the Durbar that was held Lord Curzon made the following speech. In his reply the Maharajah thus alluded among other things to Lord Curzon's work for India and its Native Princes: "It is only in the fitness of things that the closing days of your Excellency's Viceroyalty, which throughout has been distinguished for the most deep-seated sympathy for the teeming millions of India and the most passionate desire to promote their happiness, prosperity and contentment, should be marked by such an actual proof of solicitude for the welfare of one of the premier States in India." Subsequently the Maharajah came all the way from Kashmir to Bombay, a distance of 1,200 miles, to bid farewell personally to Lord Curzon.

Three times since I came to India as Viceroy have I been privileged as representative of the Government to instal an Indian Prince, but I have never before enjoyed the pleasure of conferring an enhancement or restitution of powers upon a ruling Chief, and in the annals of the Foreign Office we can discover no record of such a ceremony ever having taken place. The present occasion is therefore unique in its character as well as agreeable in its relation both to the Prince who is the recipient of the compliment and to the people who share in the honour that is being conferred upon their Ruler. This ceremony may be looked upon from a threefold point of view, either as typifying the policy of the Paramount Power, or as affecting the fortunes of the Maharaja, or the destinies of his State. Let me say a word upon all these aspects of the case.

The position which is occupied by the British Crown towards the Feudatory Princes of India is one of the greatest responsibilities that is anywhere enjoyed by a Sovereign Authority. Sometimes it may impose upon that authority unwelcome or distasteful obligations. But far more often it is the source of a relationship which is honourable and advantageous to both, and which associates them in bonds of a political union without any parallel for its intimacy or confidence in the world. As one who has represented the Sovereign Power for an unusual length of time in India, I can speak with some right to be heard when I say that anything that enhances the security or adds to the dignity of the Indian Princes is above all things welcome to the British Government. Titles and honours and salutes it is in the power of the supreme authority in many countries to bestow, and it is from no vain or childish instinct that the world in all ages has attached value to these emblems or rewards. But surely amongst them the most dignified distinction to offer and the proudest to receive must be the augmentation of governing powers bestowed upon a ruler to whom they are given, not as a matter of course, but because he has merited them by faithful devotion to the interests of his people and by loyal attachment to the Paramount Power. Such an act is even more congenial to the latter, if it marks the rescision of an attitude that may have been called for in different circumstances, but that might be thought to carry with it the suspicion of distrust. It gives me therefore the highest pleasure to be here to-day to confer this particular honour upon one of the foremost of the Indian Princes. But the pleasure is enhanced by the circumstances of the State and of the Ruler to whom it is offered.

I know not why it is, but the State of Kashmir, so fertile in all its resources, has always been more productive of strange rumours than any other Native State in India. Thus in Lord Lansdowne's day, it was widely circulated that the State was about to be taken over by the Crown. Similarly a few years ago, at the very time when I was first considering with your Highness the restoration of your powers, it was actually spread about that I was discussing with you a territorial exchange, by which the Kashmir valley should pass into the hands of the Government of India, and that the British officials were to come, even after the manner of the old Moghuls, and spend their summers at Srinagar or Gulmarg. Only the other day a fresh crop of silly rumours had to be formally denied, namely, that in handing back to you the first place in the Government of your State, we had imposed conditions as regards the tenure of property by Europeans in Kashmir, for which there was not one word of foundation. Your Highness, is not the action which I am taking to-day the most eloquent commentary upon these absurd fictions? Does it not testify in the most emphatic manner to the rectitude and good faith of the British Government? If excuses for a different policy, for a policy of escheat or forfeiture in Native States, were required, history will supply cases in which it has sometimes not been lacking. But we have deliberately set ourselves to carry out the opposite political theory, namely to retain the Native States of India intact, to prolong and fortify their separate existence, and to safeguard the prestige and authority of their rulers. Such has been our attitude towards Kashmir ever since the end of the first Sikh war, when we made over to your grandfather, already the ruler of the State of Jammu, the much more valuable possession of Kashmir. Since that day there has been no departure from this policy, and there has been no more striking evidence of it than the step which I am taking to-day, and which I consider it my good fortune that before I leave India I am in a position to take. It shows conclusively, if any further proofs were required, that it is our desire to see Kashmir and Jammu a single and compact State in the hands of a ruler qualified to represent its dignity and authority before all India.

Your Highness, there is a third reason why I have found this act so agreeable, and that is personal to yourself. Since I arrived in India, when you were the first Ruling Chief to greet me upon the steps of Government House at Calcutta, we have met on many occasions and have constantly corresponded. You have been a guest at Calcutta, and it is only a series of accidents, first the flood in 1903, and then the delay in my return from England last year, and finally the circumstances attending my departure in the present autumn, that have prevented me from enjoying the princely hospitality, that you have so frequently pressed upon me, at Srinagar. However, though these opportunities have been wanting, there have not been lacking many others, not merely of acquiring your Highness' friendship, but of forming a personal regard for yourself and a high opinion of those qualities of head and heart which will now find an even wider scope for their exercise.

I feel that I am the indirect means of honouring a Prince who will so conduct himself as to be worthy of honour and who will never cause my successors to regret the step which I have taken. The State of Kashmir is, indeed, a noble and enviable dominion of which to be the ruler. Its natural beauties have made it famous alike in history and romance, and they draw to it visitors from the most distant parts. It possesses a laborious and docile population. Its industrial resources are already growing rapidly and are capable of immense additional expansion. Its accounts have been placed in excellent order; its land settlement has been effected on equitable lines; its revenues are mounting by leaps and bounds. It is about be connected with India by a railway and will thus lose the landlocked condition, which has often been the source of economic suffering without, I hope, sacrificing the picturesque detachment that renders it so attractive to visitors. Your Highness will remember that this railway was my first official suggestion to you at Calcutta in January 1899, and though nearly seven years have since elapsed, I am pleased to think that the alignment and gauge are now fixed, the shares to be borne in the undertaking by the Government of India and the Durbar are determined, the money is forthcoming, and there only remains to commence work. Finally, your State possesses a mountain frontier unequalled in diversity of race and character of natural beauty, and in political interest, and towards its protection you make the largest contribution of any State in India to Imperial defence. I allude to the Kashmir Imperial Service troops, of which your Highness is so justly proud, and whose service to the Empire has already won for your Highness the exalted rank of a British General.

Such are the features and the prospects of the State of which your Highness is the Ruler, and of which you are now given this supreme and responsible charge. Henceforward the State Council, which for the last sixteen years has administered the affairs of the State, will cease to exist, and its powers will be transferred under proper guarantees to yourself. You will be assisted in the discharge of these duties by your brother, Raja Sir Amar Singh, who has already occupied so prominent a position in the administration, and who will be your Chief Minister and right hand man. I am convinced that he will devote his great natural abilities to your faithful service, and it will be your inclination as well as your duty to repose in him a full measure of your trust. In all important matters you will be able to rely upon the counsel and support of the British Resident, who, owing to the peculiar conditions of Kashmir, has played so important a part in the recent development of the country, and whose experience and authority will always be at your command and will assist to maintain the credit of the State. I feel convinced that your Highness will exercise your powers in a manner that will justify the Government of India for their confidence, and that will be gratifying to your people and creditable to yourself. You rule a State in which the majority of your subjects are of a different religion from the ruling caste, and in which they are deserving of just and liberal consideration. You rule a State in which the cultivating classes are poor and liable to sudden vicissitudes of fortune, so that there is frequently a call for leniency in treatment. You rule a State which is much before the eyes of the world and is bound to maintain the highest standard of efficiency and self-respect. Finally, you rule a State which has a great and splendid future before it, and which should inspire you with no higher or no lower aim, than to be worthy of the position of its ruler and thus to add fresh lustre to the proud title of Maharaja of Jammu and Kashmir.

SPEECH AT THE DALY COLLEGE, INDORE.

On November 5th, the ceremony of laying the foundation-stone of the renovated College for Chiefs and Thakurs in Central India, called after the late Sir Henry Daly, a popular Agent to the Governor-General in Central India, whose son Major Daly was present on this occasion, was performed at Indore, after which Lord Curzon was to have addressed the audience in the following speech, which was read for him, owing to his weak state of health, by Mr. S. M. Fraser, late Foreign Secretary—

Major Daly, Your Highnesses, Ladies and Gentlemen,—I have been asked to read the following speech by the Viceroy written in his own words :—

I greatly regret that a sudden attack of illness has prevented me at the last moment from coming to Indore to fulfil my long standing engagement with the Chiefs of Central India to lay the foundation stone of the new Daly College and to bid you all good-bye. I regret this both for my own sake, and also on account of the great trouble, and I fear, disappointment caused to the Princes who have gathered in such numbers at Indore to do me honour. In these circumstances I have deputed by late Foreign Secretary, Mr. Fraser, to attend at Indore on my behalf, and to read to you the remarks which I should otherwise have made myself. The following is what I had intended to say.

This is the last occasion, I imagine, on which I shall ever address an assemblage of Indian Chiefs. But it is perhaps not the least important, since we are founding or refounding, here to-day, one of those institutions in whose welfare I have always taken the deepest interest, because in their success is bound up the success of the princely class, whose sons will be educated within its walls, and who will stand or fall in the future according to the character that is in them from their birth and the shape that is given to that character by education. The old Daly College was founded here as long ago as 1881 in the time of that excellent and beloved Political Officer, Sir Henry Daly. It was a College for the scions of the princely and aristocratic classes of Central India, and it did its work, within certain limits, fairly well. But its scope was too narrow, it was not sufficiently supported by those for whom it was intended, and it gradually dwindled in numbers and utility. It became overshadowed by the Mayo College at Ajmer, and nearly four years ago, when I presided over the conference on Chiefs' Colleges at Calcutta, we all felt that the best thing to do would be, not exactly to merge the Daly College in the larger institution, but to maintain it as a feeder to the latter and to encourage the Central India Chiefs to give it their support and to send their sons for the finishing stages of their education to

Ajmer. Then two unforeseen things happened. In proportion as our interest and expenditure on the Mayo College began to strengthen and popularise that institution, turning it into a Chiefs' College worthy of the name and drawing its recruits, not from Rajputana only, but from the whole of Northern and even sometimes from Southern India, so did a spirit of emulation and pride begin to stir in the bosoms of the Central India Chiefs, and they said to themselves: "Are we merely to be the handmaid of Ajmer? Shall we not have a pukka Chiefs' College of our own? May we not revive the glories of the Daly College and prove to the world that in the modern pursuit of enlightenment and progress Central India is not going to lag behind?" The second occurrence was this: I sent Major Daly as Agent to the Governor-General to Indore, and he speedily made the discovery that the Central India Chiefs were anxious, not indeed, to withdraw their support from Ajmer, but to give it in independent and larger measure to a College of their own, and to find the money and provide the guarantees that would raise the Daly College to a level of equal dignity and influence, Imbued with natural ardour and with the additional desire to resuscitate and vindicate his father's original aim, he pushed the matter forward, as did also Mr. Bayley in the interval before he left Central India for Hyderabad, and pressed the claims of the new scheme upon the Government of India.

Thus, in the energy of these two Officers and still more in the enthusiasm and liberality of the Central India Chiefs, notably those of the wealthier States of Gwalior, Indore and Rewa, we have the origin of the movement, which we are carrying forward to-day to a further stage, and the secret of the rejuvenated Daly College, which, Phœnix-like, is about to spring from the unexhausted ashes of its predecessor and to start its new existence in the handsome and dignified setting of which I have just laid the first stone. But what, it may be asked, Your Highnesses, is this College to do for your sons? I think I know what you want, and I am sure I know what the Government of India want, and I believe that we both want the same thing. We both desire to raise up a vigorous and intelligent race of young men who will be in touch with modern progress, but not out of touch with old traditions, who will be liberally educated, but not educated out of sympathy with their own families and people, who will be manly and not effeminate, strong-minded but not strong-willed, acknowledging a duty to others instead of being a law unto themselves, and who will be fit to do something in the world instead of settling down into fops or spendthrifts or drones. How are we to accomplish this? The answer is simple. First, you must have the College properly built, properly equipped, and properly endowed. Then you must have a good staff of teachers carefully selected for their aptitudes and adequately paid, and a Principal who has a heart as well as a head for his task. Then you must have a sound curriculum, a spirit of local patriotism and a healthy tone. And finally, you must have two other factors, the constant support and patronage of the Political Officers who live in this place and in the various Central India States, and above all the personal enthusiasm, the close supervision, and the vital interest of the Chiefs themselves. I say above all, because the lesson which the Chiefs of India have to learn, if they have not learned it already, is that these Colleges will depend in the last resort not upon Government support, but upon their support, and that the future is in their hands much more than in ours.

Well, I have named rather a long list of requirements, and it contains a good many items, but there is not one of them that is not realisable by itself, and there is not the slightest reason why they should not all be realised in combination. You have a good model in the Mayo College not so far away. This meeting of to-day shows that the sympathies of the Chiefs are in the undertaking, and if only you adhere to your present spirit and temper, success should be assured. I look forward to the day as not far distant when each State, instead of having to come to the Government of India for any form of expert assistance that it may require, whether it be a Dewan, or a Councillor, or an educational officer, or an estate manager, or an officer of Imperial Service Troops, or an engineer, will have in its midst a body of young men sprung from itself, living on its soil, and devoted to its interest, who will help the Chief or the Durbar in the work of development or administration. The old-fashioned Sirdar or Thakor, who has followed the ways of his ancestors and is often unacquainted with English, will tend to disappear, and will be replaced by a younger generation with new ideals and a modern education. The change will sometimes have its drawbacks. But it is inevitable, and on the whole it will be for good. You cannot have a number of these colleges, scattered about India. There will now be four principal ones, namely those at Ajmer, Lahore. Rajkot and Indore, as well as many subsidiary institutions. You cannot turn out annually some scores of highly educated young Indian gentlemen, brought up with the sort of training that is given in these institutions without producing a far-reaching effect upon the aristocracy of India. People do not see it yet, because they hardly know what we are doing at these places or the immense strides that are being made. But in India I am always looking ahead, I am thinking of what will happen fifty years hence, and I confidently assert that from these years of active labour and fermentation there must spring results that will alter the face of Native States and will convert the Indian Nobility and land-owning classes into a much more powerful and progressive factor in the India of the future.

And now, your Highnesses, in this my message of farewell to the Indian Princes, what shall I say? They know that, throughout my term of office, one of my main objects has been to promote their welfare, to protect their interests, to stimulate their energies and to earn their esteem. Nothing in this wonderful land, which has fired the impulses and drained the strength of the best years of my life, has appealed to me more than the privilege of co-operation with the Chiefs of India, men sprung from ancient lineage, endowed with no ordinary powers and reponsibilities, and possessing nobility of character as well as of birth. It seemed to me from the start, that one of the proudest objects which the representative of the Sovereign in India could set before himself, would be to draw these rulers to his side, to win their friendship, to learn their opinions and needs, and to share with them the burden of rule. That is why I called them my colleagues and partners in the speech that I made at Gwalior six years ago, why I bade them to Delhi, and have frequently been honoured by their company at Calcutta, why I have personally installed this chief and enhanced the powers of that, have gone in and out among them, so that there is scarcely an accessible Native State in India that I have not visited, have corresponded with them and they with me, until at the end of it all, I can truthfully speak of them, not merely as colleagues and partners but as personal friends. For the same reason I am here to-day, so that almost my last official act in India may be one that brings me into contact with the princely class to whom I am so deeply attached, and who have shown me such repeated marks of their regard, never more so than during the past few weeks in connection with my approaching departure.

Your Highnesses, what is it that we have been doing together during the past seven years,—what marks or symptoms can we point to of positive advance? To me the answer seems very clear. The Chiefs have been doing a great deal and the Government have been trying to do a great deal also. When their States have been attacked by famine, the Chiefs have readily accepted the higher and more costly standards of modern administration, and the Durbars have courageously thrown themselves into the struggle. There has been a noticeable raising of the tone and quality of internal administration all round; many of the Chiefs have reformed their currency and have devoted more funds to public works and education; they have learned to husband instead of squandering their resources, and have set before themselves a high conception of duty. When we have had external wars, the Princes have freely offered assistance in troops horses and supplies. I cannot readily forget the hospital ship which that enlightened Prince, the Maharaja Scindia, who is here to-day, equipped at his own expense and took out to China. Severa of the Chiefs had volunteered their own services also. When I addressed them last year about the Imperial Service Troops, they replied to me in language of the utmost cordiality and encouragement. There have been other services that cannot be omitted. When we have internal calamity or distress, as in the case of the recent earthquake, the purses of the Chiefs are always open to help their suffering fellow-creatures in British India. Do we not all remember the princely benefaction of the Maharaja of Jaipur, who started the Indian Peoples' Famine Trust with a gift of twenty-one lakhs, which was subsequently increased by the contributions of some of his brother Chiefs. There never was a more noble or magnanimous use of great riches.

Finally, there were the splendid donations made by the Indian Princes to the Queen Victoria Memorial Fund, from which is in course of being raised, at the capital of the Indian Empire, a building worthy to bear her illustrious name.

When we began that great enterprise there were plenty of critics to scoff and jeer, and not too many to help; but now the tide has turned, The foundation stone of the main building will be laid in Calcutta in a few weeks time by the Prince of Wales, and he will see in the collection already assembled in the Indian Museum and afterwards to be transferred to the hall, such an exhibition of interesting and valuable objects as will make the Victoria Hall not only a fitting memorial to a venerated Sovereign, but a National Gallery of which all India may well be proud. During the past summer I have, as you know, addressed the majority of the Indian Princes as regards the objects to be gathered for this exhibition, and from their treasuries and armouries and toshakhanas, they have willingly produced, on gift or on loan, such a number of historical and valuable articles as will convert the Princes' Gallery of the future into a microcosm of the romance and pageantry of the East. When the Victoria Hall has been raised and equipped, the Princes will be proud of their handiwork, and there will, perhaps, be one other individual far away who will have no cause to feel ashamed.

I have described to you the work of the Princes in recent years. Let me say a word about the work of the Government. It has been our object to encourage and stimulate all those generous inclinations of which I have spoken. For this purpose we have lent to the Chiefs officers in famine times, officers for settlement, officers for irrigation programmes, officers as tutors and guardians. We would never force a European upon a Native State, but if a European is asked for or wanted, I would give the best. We have lent money on easy terms to such States as were improverished, in order to finance them in adversity, and have remitted the interest on our loans. Then there are all the educational projects of which I have spoken and of which this is one. When I look at the Chiefs' Colleges as they are now, with increased staff, with a revised curriculum, with enlarged buildings, with boys hurrying to join them, with the Chiefs eager to support them, and contrast this with the old state of affairs, the contrast is great and gratifying indeed. Then there is that favourite of my own heart, the Imperial Cadet Corps, now in existence for over three years, turning out its quota of gentlemanly and well-educated young officers, four of whom have already received commissions in the army of the King-Emperor, already acquiring its own *esprit de corps* and traditions, assisted by the framework of beautiful buildings and surroundings at Dehra Dun, and about to send its past and present members down to Calcutta to escort the son of the Sovereign in the Capital of India.

With a full heart I commit to my successor and to the Princes of India the future of the Cadet Corps, trusting to them in combination to look after it and to keep its reputation bright and its efficiency unimpaired. I am also glad to think of the encouragement that I have been able to give to the Imperial Service Troops in my time. It has fallen to me to be the first Viceroy to employ them outside of India, and though I would not have dreamed of such a step except at the earnest solicitation of the Chiefs to whom the contingents belonged, I yet regarded it as an honour to concede this fresh outlet when it was sought by their ardent patriotism. I have already mentioned the personal appeal that I addressed to all the Chiefs last year about their Imperial Service contributions, and their generous and gratifying response to it. When this matter has been settled, I hope that the Imperial Service Troops will have been placed on a firmer and broader basis than the present, without departing one iota from the sound principles that were formulated in the first place by Lord Dufferin and Lord Lansdowne more than fifteen years ago. Those principles are essential to its vitality. The Imperial Service Troops must remain the forces of the Chiefs, controlled and managed by them under the supervision of the Viceroy. They must not be swept into the Indian Army or treated as though they were the mercenaries of the Crown. They are nothing of the sort. They are the free and voluntary contributions of the Princes, and the Princes' troops they must remain. During my term of office there were also a few stumbling-blocks that it has been a source of pride to me to have assisted to remove. Foremost among these was the time-honoured difficulty about Berar, which the sagacious intelligence and the sound sense of the Nizam enabled both of us to dispose of in a manner that neither has any reason to regret. I hope also to have facilitated the solution of the difficult and complex questions that have arisen out of the Sea-Customs in Kathiawar.

There is only one other big measure that I had hoped to carry in the interest of the Chiefs in my time, but which, if it is permitted to bear fruit, I must now bequeath to my successor. I hope that he will love the Chiefs as I have done, and that they will extend to him, as I am sure that they will do, the confidence and the support which they have been good enough to give, in such generous measure, to me. As regards the particular audience whom I am now addressing, I had intended, as Major Daly knows, to make a somewhat extended tour in Central India this winter. The majority of the Central India Chiefs I have already visited, and the Maharajas of Gwalior, Orchha and Datia, the Begam of Bhopal and the Raja of Dhar have received me in their homes. The remainder I had met at Delhi or elsewhere, and had hoped to see some of them again in the course of my tour. Now that this has had to be abandoned, in consequence of my approaching departure, it has been a great compensation to me to receive your pressing invitation to come here to-day, and to meet you on such an important occasion for the last time. I may congratulate you also that, in a few days' time you will all be able to welcome their Royal Highnesses the Prince and Princess of Wales in this place. It must be gratifying to you that they are paying a special visit to Central India, and that you will all have the honour of meeting and conversing with the heir to the throne

Your Highnesses, in a fortnight from now I shall be leaving this country, and the official tie that has united me for so long to the Princes and Chiefs of India, will be snapped. No longer shall I have the official right to interest myself in their States, their administration, their people, their institutions, their families, themselves. But nothing can take away from me the recollection of the work that has been done with them. Nothing can efface the impression left upon me by their chivalryi and regard. Long may they continue to hold their great positons, secure in the affection of their own subjects and assured of the support of the Paramount Power. May they present to the world the unique spectacle of a congeries of principalities, raised on ancient foundations and cherishing the traditions of a famous past, but imbued with the spirit of all that is best and most progressive in the modern world, recognizing that duty is not the invention of the school-master but the law of life, and united in the defence of a Throne which has guaranteed their stability and is strong in their allegiance!

SPEECH ON EDUCATION.

On September 20th, Lord Curzon addressed the Directors of Public Instruction, who had assembled from the various Provinces at Simla for an Educational Conference, in the following speech, wherein he re-stated his Educational policy and reviewed the work done in the last few years under him:—

I was very much gratified when I learned that it was the desire of the Directors of Public Instruction who are assembled in Conference at Simla, that I should attend one of their meetings to say a few words of farewell. This desire was conveyed to me by Mr. Orange in language so flattering that I could not resist it, for he said that he spoke for all the Directors, and that they spoke for the whole service of which they are members. Accordingly I accepted the invitation, and that is why I am here to-day. I feel rather like a general addressing his marshals for the last time before he unbuckles his sword and retires into private life; for the task which has engaged so much of our energies during the past seven years, has been like nothing so much as a campaign marked by a long series of engagements which we have fought together, and though I am about to resign my commission, you will remain to carry on, I hope, the same colours to victory on many another well-won field. To you therefore, I need make no apology for offering a few final remarks on your own subject. It would almost be an impertinence, if I were to address you on any other. In a well-known work of fiction, one of the characters is made to groan over that bore of all bores, whose subject has no beginning, middle or end, namely, education. Here, however, where we all belong to the same category, I must accept the risk of inflicting that form of penance on others, in the hopeful assurance that I shall not be found guilty by you.

Gentlemen, when I came to India educational reform loomed before me as one of those objects which, from such knowledge of India as I possessed, appeared to deserve a prominent place in any programme of administrative reconstruction. I thought so for several reasons. In the first place, vital as is education everywhere as the instrument by which men and nations rise, yet in a country like India in its present state of development, it is perhaps the most clamant necessary of all. For here education is required not primarily as the instrument of culture, of the source of learning, but as the key to employment, the condition of all national advance and prosperity, and the sole stepping-stone for every class of the community to higher things. It is a social and political, even more than an intellectual demand, and to it alone can we look to provide a livelihcod for our citizens, to train up our public servants, to develop the economic and industrial resources of the country, to fit the people for a share in self-government which is given to them and which will increase with their deserts, and to fashion the national character on sound and healthy lines. The man in India who has grasped the education problem has got nearer to the heart of things than any of his comrades, and he who can offer to us the right educational prescription is the true physician of the State.

There is another reason for which education in India is a peculiarly British responsibility. For it was our advent in the country that brought about that social and moral upheaval of which Western education is both the symbol and the outcome. As regards religion, we sit as a Government in India, "holding no form of creed but contemplating all;" we have deliberately severed religion from politics, and though we have our own church or churches, we refrain, as an act of public policy, from incorporating Church with State. But we do not therefore lay down that ethics are, or should be, divorced from the life of the nation, or that society, because it does not rest upon dogmatic theology, should lose the moral basis without which in all ages it must sooner or later fall to pieces. For education is nothing unless it is a moral force. There is morality in secular text-books as well as in sacred texts, in the histories and sayings of great men, in the examples of teachers, in the contact between teachers and pupils, in the discipline of the class-room, in the emulation of the school life. These are the substitutes in our Indian Educational system for the oracles of Prophets or the teaching of Divines. To them we look to make India and its people better and purer. If we thought that our education were not raising the moral level, we should, none of us, bestir ourselves so gravely about it. It is because it is the first and most powerful instrument of moral elevation in India, that it must for ever remain a primary care of the State. The State may delegate a portion of the burden to private effort or to Missionary enterprise, but it cannot throw it altogether aside. So long as our Government in India is what it is, we must continue to control and to correlate educational work, to supply a large portion of the outlay, to create the requisite models and to set the tone.

As soon as I looked about me, but little investigation was required to show, in the words of a familiar quotation, that there was something rotten in the state of Denmark. For years education in India had been muddling along with no one to look after it at head-quarters or to observe its symptoms, till the men who had given up their lives to it were sick at heart and well-nigh in despair. It was not that splendid and self-sacrificing exertions had not been devoted to the task. It was not that any class, European or Indian, was indifferent to its claims; for I believe, that in India there is a genuine passion for education among all classes. It was not that there had been a deliberate or conscious neglect. But there was a deplorable lack of co-ordination. There was a vagueness as to fundamental principles. Slackness had crept in; the standards had depreciated; and what was wanting was the impulse and movement of a new life.

It was for these reasons that I threw myself, with a burning zeal, into the subject of Educational Reform. I knew the risks that had to be run. There was not one among them that could be apprehended that has not been incurred. I was aware of all the taunts that would be levelled; that we should be accused. when we were merely raising a debased standard, of wanting to shut the doors of Education in the face of the people; and when we felt it our duty to assert the proper control of Government of desiring to aggrandise the power of the State; and many other equally unfounded charges. But the object seemed to me to be worth the risk. The allies and fellow-workers were there who were only too ready and anxious to join the struggle, and it merely remained to formulate the plan of action and to go ahead.

For the first two years we surveyed the ground and reconnoitred the position of the opposing forces and then we began. I look to the meetings of the Simla Conference in the month of September 1901, just four years ago, as the first act in the real campaign. That Conference has often been denounced by those who knew not the real nature of its labours, as a sort of Star Chamber conclave, that was engaged in some dark and sinister conspiracy. Some of you were present at its meetings, and you know how much of truth there was in that particular charge. I do not hesitate to say that a Conference more independent in its character, more sincere in its aims, or more practical and far-reaching in its results, never met at the head quarters of the Indian Government. The meeting was a body of experts, non-official as well as official, convened in order to save Government from making mistakes and to assure me that we were advancing upon right lines. Our programme was laid down in the published speech with which I opened the proceedings. We covered the whole field of educational activity in our researches, and we laid down the clear and definite principles which so far from being concealed were published at full length later on in the Education Resolution of March 1904, and which, for years to come, will guide the policy of the State. Then followed the appointment of a Director-General of Education, most fully justified by the devoted labours, the informed enthusiasm and the unfailing tact of Mr. Orange. Next in order came the Universities Commission presided over by my former colleague, Sir Thomas Raleigh, in 1902. Then followed the Universities Legislation of 1903-04, of which, looking back calmly upon it, I say that I do not regret the battle or the storm, since I am firmly convinced that out of them has been born a new life for Higher Education in India. Finally came the comprehensive Resolution, of which I have spoken. Since then the policy of reform laid down by the Simla Conference has been carried into execution in every branch of educational effort, until at last the Directors of Public Instruction from every province have been sitting here for a week in Conference, to compare notes as to what has already been accomplished and discuss fresh plans for the future. These are the main landmarks of the great enterprise upon which we have all been employed for so long, and a moment has arrived when it is not impossible, to some extent, to reckon up the results.

What was the affairs that we had to redress? I will try to summarise it. As regards Primary or Elementary Education, *i.e.* Education of the children of the masses in the vernaculars, the figures which appeared in the Resolution were sufficiently significant. Four out of every five Indian villages were found to be without a school. Three out of every four Indian boys grow up without any education; only one Indian girl in every forty attends any kind of school. These figures are, of course, less appealing in a continent of the size, the vast population, the national characteristics and the present state of advancement of India, than they would be in any Western country; but they are important as illustrating, if not the inadequacy of past efforts, at any rate the immensity of the field that remains to be conquered. We found Primary Education suffering from a divergence of views as to its elementary functions and courses, and languishing nearly everywhere for want of funds. In Secondary Education we found schools receiving the privilege of recognition upon most inadequate tests, and untrained and incompetent teachers imparting a course of instruction devoid of life to pupils, subjected to a pressure of examinations that encroached upon their out-of-school hours, and was already beginning to sap the brain power as well as the physical strength of the rising generation. Inferior teaching in secondary schools, further, has this deleterious effect, that it reacts upon College work and affects the whole course of University instruction of which it is the basis and starting-point. We found these schools in many cases accommodated in wretched buildings and possessing no provision for the boarding of the pupils. As regards the vernaculars, which must for long be the sole instrument for the diffusion of knowledge among all except a small minority of the Indian people, we found them in danger of being neglected and degraded in the pursuit of English, and in many cases very bad English, for the sake of its mercantile value. By all means let English be taught to those who are qualified to learn it, but let it rest upon a solid foundation of the indigenous languages; for no people will ever use another tongue with advantage, that cannot first use its own with ease.

But in Higher Education the position was still worse: for here it was not a question so much of a blank sheet in the education of the community, as of page scribbled over with all sorts of writing, some of it well formed and good, but much of it distorted and wrong. We found in some of the affiliated Colleges a low standard of teaching and a lower of learning; ill paid and insufficient teachers, pupils crowded together in insanitary buildings, the cutting down of fees in the interests of an evil commercial competition, and management on unsound principles. Finally, coming to the Universities, we found courses of study and a system of tests which were lowering the quality while steadily increasing the volume of the human output: students driven like sheep from lecture-room to lecture-room and examination to examination, text-books badly chosen, degrees pursued for their commercial value; the Senates with over-swollen numbers selected on almost every principle but that of educational fitness, the Syndicates devoid of statutory powers,—a huge system of active but often misdirected effort, over which like some evil phantom seemed to hover the monstrous and maleficent spirit of Cram.

Of course, there were better and reassuring features in the picture and there were parts of the country where the merits greatly exceeded the defects. But we had to correct the worst, even more than to stimulate the best, and like a doctor it was our duty to diagnose the unsound parts of the body, rather than to busy ourselves with the sound. Moreover, there were some faults that were equally patent everywhere. It is recorded of the Emperor Aurungzeb, after he had seized the throne of the Moghul Empire, that he publicly abused his old tutor for not having prepared him properly for these great responsibilities. "Thus," he said, "did you waste the precious hours of my youth in the dry, unprofitable, and never-ending task of learning words." That is exactly the fault that we found with every phase of Indian Education as we examined it. Everywhere it was words that were being studied—not ideas. The grain was being spilled and squandered while the husks were being devoured. I remember a passage in the writings of Herbert Spencer in which he says that to prepare us for complete living is the true function of education. That is a conception which is perhaps as yet beyond the reach of the majority of those whom we are trying to educate in this country. But in the rut into which it had sunk, I doubt if European Education in India, as we were conducting it, could be described as a preparation for living at all, except in the purely materialistic sense, in which unhappily it was too true. But of real living, the life of the intellect, the character, the soul, I fear that the glimpses that were obtainable were rare and dim.

Of course, all these tendencies could not be corrected straight away. It would be a futile and arrogant boast to say that we have reformed Indian Education. There is equal scope for educational reformers now, to-morrow, next day and always. Education is never reformed. It may advance, or remain stationary, or recede. It may also advance on right lines, or on wrong lines. Our claim is merely to have rescued it from the wrong track, and given it a fresh start on the right one. If we have set up a few milestones on the path of true progress, we shall have done something for it and perhaps made further advance easier for our successors.

What I think we may claim to have effected has been the following. In primary education we have realised that improvement means money. We have laid down that Primary Education must be a leading charge on provincial revenues, and in order to supply the requisite impetus, we gave in our last budget a very large permanent annual grant of 35 lakhs, to be devoted to that purpose alone. This will be the real starting-point of an advance that ought never to be allowed henceforward to slacken. Most of the money will go in building to begin with, and a good deal in maintenance afterwards. Thousands of new primary schools are already opening their doors under these auspices, and in a few years' time the results should be very noteworthy. In building we lay stress upon the provision of suitable and airy school-houses, in place of the dark rooms or squalid sheds in which the children had previously been taught. Training schools for teachers are similarly springing up or being multiplied in every direction. We have defined the nature of the object lessons that ought to be taught to the children in Primary Schools and the courses of study and the books that are required for the instruction of the cultivating class. We have everywhere raised the pay of primary teachers where this was inadequate, and are teaching them that their duty is to train the faculties of their pupils and not to compel them to the listless repetition of phrases in which the poor children find no meaning. I look as the result of this policy to see a great development in Elementary Education in the near future. It is apt to be neglected in India in favour of the louder calls and the more showy results of Higher Education. Both are equally necessary, but in the structure of Indian society one is the foundation and the other the coping stone ; and we who are responsible must be careful not to forget the needs of the voiceless masses, while we provide for the interests of the more highly favoured minority who are better able to protect themselves.

In Secondary Education the faults were largely the same, and the remedies must be the same. Also more teachers are the first desideratum, more competent teachers the second, more inspectors the third. The increase that we have everywhere effected in the inspecting staff is remarkable. Next comes reform in courses of study and buildings. All these necessities are summed up in the duty which we have undertaken of laying down sound tests for official recognition. From this we pass on to the development of the commercial and industrial sides of these schools as against the purely literary, since there are thousands of boys in them who must look to their education to provide them with a practical livelihood rather than to lead them to a degree ; and above all to the reduction of examinations. That is the keynote everywhere, Have your tests, sift out the good from the bad, furnish the incentive of healthy competition, but remember that the Indian boy is a human being with a mind to be nurtured and a soul to be kept alive : and do not treat him as a mechanical drudge, or as a performing animal which has to go at stated intervals through the unnatural task to which its trainer has laboriously taught it to conform.

I hope that the Government of India will not be indifferent to the claims of Secondary Education in the future. When the Universities and the Colleges have been put straight, we must look to the feeders and these feeders are the High Schools. Indeed, we cannot expect to have good Colleges without good Schools. I am not sure, if a vote were taken among the intelligent middle classes of this country, that they would not sooner see money devoted to Secondary Education than to any other educational object. The reason is that it is the basis of all industrial or professional occupation in India. There is just a danger that between the resonant calls of Higher Education and the pathetic small voice of Elementary Education the claims of Secondary Education may be overlooked, and I therefore venture to give it this parting testimonial.

When we come to Higher Education, our policy, though based on identical principles, assumes a wider scope, and has, I hope, already effected an even more drastic change. It is very difficult to carry out substantial reforms in Higher Education in India, because of the suspicion that we encounter among the educated classes that we really desire to restrict their opportunities and, in some way or other, to keep them down. There is, of course, no ground whatever for suspicion. Not only does it run counter to the entire trend of British character and to all the teachings of British history, but it would be a short-sighted and stupid policy even if it were adopted. For Education, to whatever extent it may be directed or controlled, is essentially an organic and not an artificial process; and no people, particularly a highly intelligent and ambitious people like the educated classes in India, could possibly be confined, so to speak, in a particular educational compartment or chamber, because the Government was foolish enough to try and turn the key upon them. What has been in our minds, though it has not always been easy to explain it to others, has been firstly, the conviction that those who were getting Higher Education were getting the wrong sort of it, because they were merely training the memory at the expense of all the other faculties of the mind, and that it could not be good for a nation that its intellect should be driven into these lifeless and soulless grooves; and secondly, the belief that reform was to be sought by making educationalists more responsible for Education in every department, giving them power on Senates and Syndicates, improving the quality of the teaching staff, and providing for the expert inspection of Colleges and Schools. Let me put it in a sentence: Higher Education ought not to be run either by politicians or by amateurs. It is a science, the science of human life and conduct, in which we must give a fair hearing and a reasonable chance to the Professor.

If our reforms are looked at in this light, it will be seen that they are based upon a uniform and logical principle. We swept away the old overgrown Senates or bodies of Fellows, and reconstituted them on lines which should make educational interests predominate in the government of the Universities. Similarly, we placed experts in the majority on the executive committees, or Syndicates. It is these bodies who will draw up the new courses, prescribe the text-books and frame the future standards of education. Of course, they may go wrong, and Government retains the indispensable power of putting them right if they do so. But the initial and principal responsibility is theirs, and if they cannot make a better thing of Higher Education in India, then no one can. Similarly, we carry the expert into the *mofussil*. If we are to improve the affiliated institutions, we must first prescribe, as we have done, sound and definite conditions of affiliation, and then we must send round sympathetic inspecting officers to detect local shortcomings, to offer advice and to see that the new conditions are observed. Simultaneously, if sustained efforts are made, as we are making them, to improve the quality of the teachers and give them opportunities when on furlough of studying other systems; and if at the other end of the scale, we provide for the proper entertainment of the boys in well-managed hostels, or boarding houses, then it seems to me that we have created both the constitutional and the academic machinery by which reform can be pursued, and that if it be not accomplished it must be for some reason which we have failed to discern. Anyhow, I can see nothing in the objects or processes that I have described to which the most sensitive or critical of Indian intelligences need object; and the most hopeful guarantee of success is to be found, in my view, in the fact that the best and most experienced Indian authorities are entirely on our side.

Personally, therefore, I regard our University legislation and the reform that will spring from it as a decree of emancipation. It is the setting free for the service of Education, by placing them in authoritative control over Education, of the best intellects and agencies that can be enlisted in the task, and it is the casting off, and throwing away of the miserable gyves and manacles that had been fastened upon the limbs of the youth of India, stunting their growth, crippling their faculties, and tying them down. In my view we are entitled to the hearty co-operation of all patriotic Indians in the task, for it is their people that we are working for and their future that we are trying to safeguard and enlarge. Already I think that this is very widely recognised. The old cries have, to a large extent, died away. Among the valedictory messages and tributes, which I have received in such numbers from native sources during the past few weeks, have been many which placed in the forefront the services which I am generously credited with having rendered to the cause of Indian Education. One of the most gratifying features in this renascence in the history of Indian education, as I hope it may in time deserve to be called, has been the stimulus given to private liberality, showing that Indian Princes and noblemen are keenly alive to the needs of the people and are in cordial sympathy with the movement that we have striven to inaugurate. The Raja of Nabha called upon the Sikh community to rouse themselves and put the Khalsa College at Amritsar on a proper footing for the education of their sons, and they responded with contributions of 20 lakhs. In Bengal there have been handsome gifts for the proposed new College at Ranchi. The Aligarh Trustees continue to improve their magnificent College, and, last year, I believe, achieved a record subscription list in their Conference at Lucknow. In the United Provinces the enthusiasm of Sir J. La Touche, has kindled a corresponding zeal in others. The College at Bareilly is to be shifted from a corner of the High School buildings to a new building on a fine site, given by the Nawab of Rampur. When I was at Lucknow in the spring, I saw the site of the new residential College in the Badshah Bagh, to which the Maharaja of Balrampur has given a donation of three lakhs. Government has not been behindhand in similar liberality; and apart from the 25 lakhs which we promised and are giving to assist the Universities in the work of reconstruction, we have assisted the purchase of sites for University buildings in many places, and are prepared to help them in other ways. It is a truism in Higher Education, as elsewhere, that the first condition of progress is money, and this is being provided both by Government and by private effort in no stinted measure.

I might detain you, Gentlemen, much longer by discussing the various measures that we have taken with regard to other branches of Education in India, for it is to be confessed that the aspirations which I set before myself and before the Simla Conference were not confined to the sphere of Primary, Secondary and Higher Education alone, but embraced the whole field of educational reform. There is no corner of it where we have not laboured and are not labouring. We have not in our zeal for Indian Education forgotten the cause of European and Eurasian Education in this country; we have revised the Code, we have made a most careful examination of the so-called Hill Schools, and are re-establishing the best among them on an assured basis. We are giving handsome grants-in-aid and scholarships. We are appointing separate inspectors for these institutions and are starting a special Training College for teachers.

Then there is a class of Education, which deserves and has attracted our particular attention viz., that which is intended to qualify its recipients for the professional occupations of Indian life. Here our Agricultural College at Pusa, which is intended to be the parent of similar institutions in every other province, each equipped with a skilled staff and adequate funds, has been specially devised to provide at the same time thorough training in all branches of agricultural science and practical instruction in estate management and farm work. These instructions will, I hope, turn out a body of young men who will spread themselves throughout India, carrying into the management of states and estates, into private enterprise, and into Government employ, the trained faculties with which their college courses will have supplied them. Agriculture in India is the first and capital interest of this huge continent, and agriculture, like every other money-earning interest, must rest upon Education.

Neither have we forgotten Female Education, conscious that man is to a large extent what woman makes him, and that an educated mother means educated children. Since the Simla Conference, Bengal has already doubled the number of girls under instruction. The female inspecting staff has been overhauled in most provinces, and some ladies possessing high qualifications have been sent out from England. Good model girls' schools and good training schools for the female teachers are a desideratum everywhere. It will take a long time to make substantial progress, but the forward movement has begun.

There remains the subject of Technical Education which has occupied an immense amount of our attention both at the Simla Conference and ever since. We have had Commissions and reports and enquiries. We have addressed Local Governments and studied their replies. But we are only slowly evolving the principles under which Technical Instruction can be advantageously pursued in a country where the social and industrial conditions are what they are in India. Whether we look at the upper or at the lower end of the scale, this difficulty is equally apparent. People wonder why Mr. Tata's Institute of Science comes so slowly into being, and in a country where it is the custom to attribute anything that goes wrong to the Government, all sorts of charges have been brought against us of apathy or indifference or obstruction. No one would more readily acknowledge than Mr. Tata himself that, so far from discouragement or opposition, he met with nothing at the hands of Government but sympathy and support. But Mr. Tata wisely wants not merely to start the magnificent conception of his father, but to make it practical and to ensure its success, and I can assure you that the rival views that prevail as to the best method of accommodating this great idea to the necessities of India are extraordinary. We have experienced similar difficulties in our own smaller undertakings. As is generally known, we have instituted a number of technical scholarships of £150 each for Indian students in Europe and America; but, strange as it may seem, it has not invariably been easy, at first, to find the candidates to fill them. However, we now have a number of Indian scholars from Bengal, who are studying mining at Birmingham, and our latest step was to grant three scholarships for Textile Industries in Bombay. Other attempts will follow, and in a short time there will, in my view, be no lack either of candidates or subjects. Similarly with Industrial Schools, which we have been anxious to start on a large scale for the practical encouragement of local industries, there is the widest diversity of opinion as to the principles and the type. For it must be remembered, that although India is a country with strong traditions of industrial skill and excellence, with clever artisans and with an extensive machinery of trade guilds and apprentices, these are constituted upon a caste basis which does not readily admit of expansion, while the industries themselves are, as a rule, localised and small, rendering co-ordination difficult. We are, however, about to make an experiment on a large scale in Bombay and Bengal, and I have every hope that upon the labours and researches of the past few years posterity will be able to build.

Upon these, and many other subjects, I might discourse to you at length. But you are better acquainted with them than I am, and I have addressed myself to-day, not so much to details as to the principles that have underlain the great movement of educational activity, upon which we have together been engaged. To you and to your successors I must now commit the task. It is a work which may well engage your best faculties and be the proud ambition of a lifetime. On the stage where you are employed there is infinite scope for administrative energy, and what is better for personal influence: while in the background of all your labours, stands the eternal mystery of the East with its calm and immutable traditions, but its eager and passionate eyes. What the future of Indian Education may be, neither you nor I can tell. It is the future of the Indian Race, in itself the most hazardous though absorbing of speculations. As I dream of what Education in India is to be or become, I recall the poet's lines:

> "Where lies the land to which the ship would go?
> Far, far ahead is all her seamen know.
> And where the land she travels from? Away
> Far, far behind is all that they can say."

In the little space of navigable water for which we are responsible between the mysterious past and the still more mysterious future, our duty has been to revise a chart that was obsolete and dangerous, to lay a new course for the vessel and to set her helm upon the right tack.

SPEECH AT THE PILGRIMS' DINNER, LONDON, ON APRIL 6, 1906.

Lord Curzon was entertained after his return to England at a dinner given in his honour by the Pilgrims in London. Lord Roberts presided, and Lord George Hamilton, who was Secretary of State for India during the greater part of Lord Curzon's rule as Viceroy, proposed his health, after which His Lordship replied in the following speech which may be said to be his last farewell to India and its Viceroyalty:

I need hardly assure you that I appreciate most highly the great honour which you have conferred upon me this evening, and the manner in which you have just received the toast of my health. If a pilgrim is still, as he always used to be, a person who wanders abroad for a definite object at a distance from his native land, then as a wanderer of this character for many years I may perhaps claim that there is something not inappropriate in my being entertained by a Society of Pilgrims. And if, as I understand, this particular association of pilgrims, who are gathered round these tables, consists of Englishmen and Americans who are banded together to promote goodwill between these two great wandering races—or perhaps I should rather say between these two great branches of the same wandering race, because, after all, English and Americans are now and henceforward one,—then may I not claim a further justification in the fact that the best pilgrimage I ever made in my life was to the other side of the water in order to persuade an American pilgrim to execute a life pilgrimage in my company? I was not the first Governor-General of India to take this prudent step. Nearly 100 years ago there was another Governor-General—Lord Wellesley—who also married an American woman, but who only did so after he had returned from India, and in the latter part of his life, when the union of which I speak happened too late to exercise any influence upon his Indian career.* I, wiser in my generation, took the step

* Marquess Wellesley married in 1825, twenty years after his administration of India, as his second wife, Marianne Caton, of Baltimore, U. S. A., who was the grand-daughter of the American patriot Carrol of Carrolstown, who was one of the signatories of the Declaration of Independence. His first wife, whom he had married in 1794, was a Frenchwoman named Hyacinthe Roland. She died in 1816. *Vide* Pearce, *Memoirs of Wellesley*, Vol. III. p. 387, Vol. I. p. 127-8.

earlier in the day, with what consequences in my administration the speech of Lord George Hamilton has sufficiently shown.

But, my lords and gentlemen, there are, I think, other connections between America and India less accidental than the matrimonial sagacity or the matrimonial felicity whichever it be—of two Governors-General nearly a century apart. I have always heard that when Christopher Columbus discovered America he was in reality on the look-out for an eastern extension of India, and it was that particular discovery that he thought he had made. Hence those extraordinary solecisms of the West Indies and the North American Indians which we continue to employ at the present day. From this point of view America may, I think, be described as a sort of historical and geographical afterthought of India, although perhaps this is an aspect of the case upon which it will not be wise for me to lay too much stress upon the present hospitable occasion. But there are other links, I think, between America and India that are closer still. In India we have been engaged for 150 years or more in making with greater or less success—I myself think with greater—the same experiment which America is undertaking in another part of the same continent, and in which we who have served in India or been resident in India wish her the good fortune which we have enjoyed. A little earlier in the evening we drank the toast of "The Sovereign of the British Empire and the President of the United States." I have often thought myself that, although there is the greatest difference in the world between the constitutions of America and India, yet there is a greater similarity between the positions of the President of the United States and the British official who is placed in charge of the destinies of India, than there is between the position of any two political functionaries in the world. Both hold their office for a limited term, both exercise, as Lord George Hamilton has pointed out, an immense authority, and have the power of exerting a great, and let us hope beneficent, influence over vast multitudes of their fellow-men, both have higher authorities above or behind them with which sometimes they are so unfortunate as to disagree—in the one case there is the Senate of the United States and the House of Representatives, and in the other case there is the Secretary of State and his Majesty's Government,—both when they descend from their official pedestals relapse into the tranquil obscurity of private citizenship, and from having been the man at the helm become that apotheosis of commonplace the man in the street. Of course the President of the United States occupies a greater position, for he is the elected ruler of a self-governing people of his own race, and that perhaps the mightiest people in the universe. But I am not sure that the Governor-General of India has not in his time had the opportunity of exercising an even greater influence over those who are committed to his charge; for he has been placed in custody for the time being of the lives and fortunes, as we have had pointed out to us, of nearly 300,000,000 of human beings, or approximately one-fifth of the human race—and they are not one people, one community, one language, one race, or one religion, they are a continent, an empire, almost a universe. They are people who, in the dispensation of Providence, have been handed over to the dominion of the British power with all the romance and wonder of their amazing history, with all the problems which come up before us for solution from day to day, and with the infinite mystery of their unknown future. My lords and gentlemen. I own that when I speak about India before any assembly I can scarcely avoid the language of emotion. I was reading the other day in one of the newspapers that as many as 400.000,000 of the population of the world were the subjects of the British Crown. That is an amazing reflection, in itself a fact which makes one pause and think. But when you remember that three out of every four of these subjects of the King are in India that Calcutta, the capital of India, is the next city in size to London in the whole British Empire, that, with the possible exception of China, India is the largest and most populous political aggregation in the universe, then I think you begin to realize to what extent the British Empire is an Asiatic empire, and how, if we cut out the Asiatic portion of it, it would infallibly dwindle in scale and in importance. I sometimes like to picture to myself this great Imperial fabric as a huge structure like some Tennysonian "Palace of Art," of which the foundations are in this country, where they have been laid and must be maintained by British hands, but of which the Colonies are the pillars, and high above all floats the vastness of an Asiatic dome.

Think of the nature of the human mechanism with which we maintain this great possession! When I was in India I had certain inquiries made with regard to our officials, applying the test of salaries, than which I know no better test or distinction between higher and lower appointments. We find that there are only 1,200 official Englishmen in India drawing salaries of £800 or over £800 a year; while of those drawing £60 or more than £60 a year, which is going very low, we find there are only 6,500 English officials in India. In other words there is but one English official to every 140,000 natives. These figures, eloquent in their simple condensation, explain how it is that none of us who have been engaged in the work of administration in India can speak of it without exultation or abandon it without regret. I am sure there are many persons at this table who share to the full the feeling which I am now expressing. If I were to ask the illustrious Field-Marshal who is presiding to-night, what has been the part of his great and eminent career of which he is most proud, I am certain he would reply in the title which his own literary labours have rendered classical—"Forty-One Years in India." If I were then to turn to Lord George Hamilton, whose official connection with India in England was greater than that of any living statesman, and who conducted the administration of India with an urbanity and sympathy which made it a positive delight to serve under him, and if I were to ask him what is the most valuable experience that he has acquired in his long and distinguished official career, I am sure he would say his connexion with India.

The soldier serving in India would say there is no soldiering like it—so earnest, so instinct with actuality. The Indian Civil servant would say there is no administration in the world so efficient and so unselfish as that of India. Their experience is my experience also. There is no one who has served in India who regrets one day or one hour that was given to it. Whatever of health or strength one may have sacrificed to it, and the sacrifice sometimes is not inconsiderable, we have gladly rendered it. And though when we come back to this country we occasionally find that nobody quite knows where we have been and still less what we have been doing, we feel that our experience in India, whatever it may have been, is something with which we would not part for anything else the world has to offer, and that we have played a part, however humble, in the greatest work that can be given to human beings.

The other day when I was thinking over what I should say at this dinner to-night. I took up a book about India to acquire some information to lay before this assembly. In it there was an article about the work and position of the Viceroy. When I read it to you you will realize how far fiction can be carried from facts. "The Viceroy of India leads a pleasant life, having a charming summer residence in a lovely mountain retreat, with the full prestige of representing the British Crown and provided with a splendid personal staff and furnished with a luxurious railway carriage ready to convey him to his Calcutta Palace in the winter, or to waft him about among beautiful landscapes and old historic cities. He is always in the prime of life, assisted by Councillors who act as his Ministers in the different departments and relieve him of all responsibility in administrative details. In the charge of the Army he is aided by the experienced officer who commands the Indian Forces." Generally speaking, the whole of that is true, individually true. I profited by every one of those advantages. And yet it is impossible to imagine a paragraph which, though the individual items of it may be correct, could give a more inadequate description of the position of the Viceroy. I read in a speech that was made by a member of the present House of Commons that the administration of India was one of pomp and pageantry. The observation appears to have captivated even the sagacious intellect of the present Secretary for India. Such is the baleful influence that is exercised by alliteration on the literary mind. I turn to the speech which has just been delivered by Lord George Hamilton, and say, "There is my answer." It is perfectly true that we did celebrate with becoming pomp and dignity the Coronation of King Edward at Delhi, and I thank Heaven that that there is one part of the Empire that is not so drab and colourless as this dingy and grimy section of the realm. I do not think there was much pomp and pageantry in the part of the life of the Viceroy that was described by Lord George Hamilton. I remember working through the long hours of the day and far into the night. I count the working days of the Viceroy as 365 in the year, if not more; and if my friend Mr. Winston Churchill were here this evening I should have to present him with this description of the life of the Viceroy, and of my administration in particular, as a more striking example of terminological inexactitude than anything that has yet been achieved by the party of which he is so distinguished an ornament. Lord George Hamilton referred to the discussion on the education question which was held at Simla, and was kind enough to point out that the 150 resolutions passed by the Conference were framed by myself. I am afraid there was the suspicion of autocracy in that assertion. The resolutions were not 150 but 175. And more remarkable still, whether they were drawn up by myself or not, every one was passed by the unanimous vote of the whole of the gentlemen seated at the table. May I commend that as a study in administrative methods to his Majesty's present advisers? There was only one other passage in the speech to which I shall allude. Lord George Hamilton paid me the greatest compliment which it is possible to pay to any man in my post by drawing a comparison between the administration of Lord Dalhousie and that of myself. Since Warren Hastings, I regard him as incomparably the greatest administrator ever charged with the destinies of India—as having an administrative genius greater almost than that of any other Englishman of our time, though perhaps I ought to say that he was a Scotsman. Had he lived and devoted his genius to the service of his country, it must have lifted him to the first rank of English statesmen. While I regard the comparison as a compliment, therefore, I cannot help finding in Lord Dalhousie's experience a sad omen; and I only hope that there may await me in future a different fate from that which befell him—coming back worn out in the exercise of his great duties and incapable of giving to his country at home that which he had given to it abroad, and wasting away in retirement the few years which should have fulfilled the supreme ambition of his existence.

I believe that when a proconsul returns from abroad he is permitted for a short period to philosophize for the benefit of his countrymen. I am not sure that sometimes his experience does not make a very great call upon any resources of philosophy that he may possess. If I were asked to sum up what were the lessons which Eastern government had given me, I should say they were these. In the first place, remember always that you are not in India or in any foreign dependency, any more than the Americans are in the Philippines, for the benefit of what in diplomacy is called your own "nationals." You are there for the benefit of the people of the country. In the old conception of colonies and dependencies the people did not occupy a prominent part. They were a mere physical feature of the country—an ethnographic excrescence on the surface of the soil. In school-days we used to read of the Roman Empire and its colonies, and how the Roman Government ended its letters to its proconsuls with the words "Si tu exercitusque valetis, bene est." Now we add to "exercitus," or substitute for it where we can, the word "populusque." That is the spirit in which all administration of dependencies which is to succeed must be carried on. That is the spirit in which South Africa was administered by Lord Milner. It is the spirit in which Egypt is being administered by Lord Cromer. It is the spirit in which India has been administered by a long succession of Viceroys and in which, I hope, it will continue to be administered. The second thing I would wish to say to high officers of State and the members of the Government is this. As far as you can, trust the man on the spot. Do not weary or fret or nag him with your superior wisdom. They are loyal to you—do not have any fear about that. They are running your show, not their own. They claim no immunity from errors of opinion or judgment, but their errors are nothing to be compared to yours. Still less do they claim any immunity from supervision and control. They know perfectly the part that is played in the Constitution by the Imperial Government and the Parliament of this country. I have often heard of "a prancing proconsul." I have never myself known a proconsul to prance, except in a Radical peroration. But, after all, remember that these men know more of the local facts than you can do yourself, and that their judgment, on the whole, is likely to be more correct. Thirdly, never sacrifice a subject interest—that is, the interest of a subject dependency or possession—to exclusively British interests. Do not force upon your dependencies a policy which may be distasteful or unsuitable to them, merely because it is advantageous to yourselves. The meaning of empire is not to impose on dependencies the will of the Mother Country or master power, but to effect a harmonious co-ordination of the interests of the whole. I read in the papers this morning that last night a member of Parliament said that the British Empire could get on very well without Natal or West Ham. I cannot personally speak for West Ham. It is just conceivable to me that the Empire might survive its loss. But Natal, no! And why? Because if you lose one colony like Natal, the process does not end there, but goes on, and you find before long that you have lost the British Empire itself. Lastly, I would say both to our own people and to all other peoples who may be engaged in empire making, send out to this task the best men you can tempt or train—send them out to India, to Egypt, to South Africa, to West Africa, to the uttermost ends of the earth. Do not be frightened by distance. Do not let them be dismayed by exile. In far-off lands, amidst alien peoples, in unfriendly solitudes, under burning suns, your sons, the offspring of your race, will still do good work, work that is good for themselves, good for the country that has sent them out, and good for the community in which they are placed. They will lead clean and healthy lives and have opportunities for doing noble and unselfish deeds. Wherever the unknown lands are waiting to be opened up, wherever the secrets or treasures of the earth are waiting to be wrested from her, wherever peoples are lying in backwardness or barbarism, wherever new civilizations are capable of being planted or old civilizations of being revived, wherever advance is possible and duty and self-sacrifice call—there is, as there has been for hundreds of years, the true summons of the Anglo-Saxon races. May we hope, in this assemblage of Englishmen and Americans, that neither of the two great branches of the Anglo-Saxon race, now so happily reunited, may ever fall below the dignity of our high calling.

PART II.

ESSAYS.

CONTENTS.

LORD CURZON.*

Lord Curzon has resigned the high post which he has held for nearly seven years amid almost universal regret, and Lord Minto is appointed to succeed him. It cannot be said that in this case an Amurath an Amurath succeeds, for it would be hard to find another ruler who combines in himself all those qualities, mental and moral, which Lord Curzon brought to his difficult task of governing this vast country, really a continent, with its three hundred millions of widely differing races and creeds. It is no disrespect to the new-comer to say that he does not possess the genius with which his predecessor is gifted without doubt. In the eyes of common-place men this will perhaps be his greatest qualification. The Ministry that have selected him do not, it seems, want in this post a brilliant man of genius with the courage of his convictions to withstand the new policy they are forcing on this country of military autocracy, but require merely one who can subserviently carry out this policy without saying nay to any demand of the Commander-in-Chief, provided he makes it in the name of that new shibboleth, which has gained currency since the Boer War, military efficiency. Whether Lord Minto is the proper person to play this subordinate part which the Ministry seem to have marked out for him, or whether when once fairly installed in the post he will not rise to its full height and refuse to carry out Lord Kitchener's commands, even like his immediate predecessor, remains to be seen. He has one thing in his favour: he has an hereditary and almost family interest in India. His great-grandfather, the first Earl of Minto, held, nearly a century ago, the high and responsible post to which his illustrious descendant has been now called. His great-grand-uncle, Sir Hugh Elliot, the brother of the first Earl, was ruler of Madras. His maternal grandfather was a famous Commander-in-Chief of Madras, Sir Thomas Hislop, who helped greatly to render the rule of the Marquis of Hastings famous by his brilliant victory of Mehidpore over Scindia; whilst several Elliots have served or are serving still in the Civil and Military services of this country. He himself is no stranger to India, having served in the second Afghan War a quarter of a century ago. He served under Lord Roberts there and also was Private Secretary to him when that great soldier went to South Africa in 1881, only, however, to return without even landing there, as an inglorious peace had hurriedly been made by Mr. Gladstone, a peace that he was destined later to avenge by his splendid victories. He may thus be supposed to share Lord Roberts' views on the present regrettable incident between the Viceroy and the Commander-in-Chief; and these views, as declared in his great speech in the House of Lords, are decidedly against Lord

---

* Calcutta Review, October, 1905.

Kitchener's pretensions, though he himselt once filled the same high post as the latter and might naturally be supposed to sympathise with him.

Though these are good auguries, one expects troublous times during the coming years of Lord Minto's Viceroyalty. Lord Kitchener requires an exceptionally strong Viceroy to control him in the militarism which will now grow very aggressive after the first easy victory just scored. Where Lord Curzon has failed one need not be called too pessimistic if he does not expect Lord Minto to succeed. The very circumstances under which he has been appointed probably tend to show that he is not meant to succeed. The present Ministry is at the very end of its career of office. The alliance with Japan has been just renewed for another ten years, and thus the only cause, which, according to its own showing, prevented it from resigning, is removed. The appointment of a new Viceroy by such a Ministry must have been made with the full consent and co-operation of the other party which is very likely to come into power next. Otherwise there may be a repetition of the untoward events of 1835, when Lord Heytesbury, who had been appointed Governor-General by an outgoing party, was a few months later told by the party that succeeded it not to proceed to India, and his appointment was cancelled under humiliating circumstances by the sending out of Lord Auckland, the choice of the party that had come into power. (*Vide* Thornton, *Hist. of British India*, Vol. VI., pp. 22-50.) The ostensible reason for this was that Lord Heytesbury was known to be very intimate with the Czar Nicholas I. of Russia. (Dr. R. Garnett in *East and West*, August, 1905, p. 798.) But the real reason was that the new Ministry wanted to carry out its preconcerted policy of aggression, which in the end proved so futile and disastrous, in Afghanistan and Central Asia, and for that purpose sent out its own Governor-General with the express mandate of wantonly interfering in Afghan matters and of thus checking, as it thought, Russian intrigues. Otherwise, the fact that Lord Heytesbury was intimate with the Czar would have been in his favour, as he would have carried on the negotiations involved by the supposed intrigues of Russia on the Indian frontier, amicably, and brought them to a peaceable issue which the new Ministry deliberately avoided. It may be taken for granted that Lord Minto has not allowed himself to be put in the humiliating position of Lord Heytesbury, and that he will continue to be the Viceroy under the Liberals also. The advent of the Liberals, however much it may be wished for by the Young India party here, bodes nothing good in the matter of the dispute between the Viceroy and the Commander-in-Chief. Lord Kitchener is the chosen pet of the Liberal party, and Lord Rosebery has often in his speeches paraded him as the heaven-sent saviour of the nation and extolled his schemes of re-organization of the Army. One therefore cannot look for relief from this quarter. The military incubus will sit tighter upon poor India and exhaust her treasury.

Only in one case does one see relief. Lord Rosebery and his followers may see reason to recall Lord Kitchener, not in disgrace but in triumph, and set him the task of re-organising the Army in England, which from all recent accounts, has been made a mess of, giving him the free hand, devoid of any control, that he so much hankers after. No one in India, not even Young Bengal which from interested motives is now exultantly jubilant over his triumph, would grudge England the glorious services of her great, her "only general," and most would join in wishing him godspeed. That would be the best solution for India of the present difficulty, and then Lord Minto would reign without the danger of being overshadowed by an imperious personality who would brook no brother near the throne. Or if the English nation is so very willing to try the experiment of giving full sway to military autocracy—not, however, on herself but on the *corpore vili* of poor India,—why is not Lord Kitchener at once made Viceroy and Governor-General as well as Commander-in-Chief, as in former times Lords Wellesley and Hastings were Commanders-in-Chief as well as Governors-General? In those days the military situation was considered so critical that to the Civil ruler was also entrusted military authority. At the present day, in the opinion of the English Ministry, things are supposed to have come to such a pass that the Civil authority must be rendered perfectly subordinate to the Military. *Silent leges inter arma* was a sound maxim. But now, it seems, laws of control and check ought to be silent in times of profound peace. It would, in the long run, be better to hold the post of Viceroy in abeyance for a time than to degrade this supreme office, which ought to be second to none in this country, by rendering it subordinate, for that is what the resignation of Lord Curzon really means. He has risen to the full height of his great character when he has proudly declined to hold this "Imperial appointment, which is the greatest honour England has to give, except the Government of herself," on any terms inconsistent with its supreme controlling power. It has been his misfortune that he hands over to his successor this high post shorn of an essential part of its power. But it is his misfortune only; he has had no hand in bringing about this diminution of the Viceregal authority. He has resigned rather than submit to it. He had but a few months more of office here. In any case he was to have left our shores next April. He goes a few months earlier now, a fact which affects him personally but little. A few months more or less of office are a matter of indifference to such a high-souled man as Lord Curzon has abundantly shown himself to be.

The renewal of his term of office last year was not of his seeking. His continuance in India has been a sacrifice of his ambitions which, as we all know, lie towards English politics. But he has sacrificed these ambitions to his sense of duty towards the Empire and towards India in particular. He had undertaken several tasks in the best interests of the land and its peoples, and those best able to judge knew that his presence here was required if they were to be brought successfully to a close. In this sense, and with this object, he consented to come out again for a fresh term. That he leaves now some of those objects unacccomplished or but half accomplished is through no fault of his own. The responsibility of placing him in circumstances where no alternative was possible but resignation, lies on other shoulders. There are occasions when a statesman must relinquish the noblest aims for higher considerations and in preference to principles from which he cannot swerve. Nobody can doubt that such a rare occasion arose in the case in which Lord Curzon found himself placed. And melancholy as are the circumstances under which so splendid a Viceroyalty has ended somewhat prematurely, one cannot but rejoice that he was found equal to the occasion and has acquitted himself during this crisis in a manner worthy of his past career and of the best traditions of English statesmanship. He did not stoop to palter for power. Nor, on the other hand, did he assume an unpractical and uncompromising attitude under a mistaken notion of duty, as sometimes happens. He did not resign at once, but tried to bring round the Ministry by conceding something in order to save the principle, in which he was throughout firm as a rock, of the final controlling authority of the Viceroy in military matters. But when he saw clearly that it was the settled purpose of the Ministry to give *carte blanche* to Lord Kitchener and to raise him above the control of the Viceroy, he recognised manfully that further opposition on his part would be useless, and refused to be a party to such a strange departure from constitutional methods.

Those who affect to see in Lord Curzon's resignation nothing but personal pique and resentment at the tactless conduct of Mr. Brodrick, do gross injustice to him and show a strange want of knowledge of his character. If the present writer has read his character aright, not so much from his words as his works, a high sense of duty must be said to form its strongest feature. Duty first to England and then to India has inspired his whole policy and every act which he has done in furtherance of that policy. Sometimes he might have been mistaken in his notions of that duty. Those of my countrymen who have first blamed him and then abused him, till now they have come to hate him as if he were their worst enemy, are eminently unreasonable, and therefore it is useless to argue with them. But to those Indians who admit that he did some good to India but did also great harm by his retrogressive measures, it may be pointed out that they are judging by a false standard and from a different point of view to that of men like Lord Curzon. With men like him England is and ought to be first and foremost in their affections: their duty is and ought to be towards England first and foremost. It is their dearest object to make England's Empire over the world stronger and wider, and their first notion of duty is to help that object forward. Now Indians, because they are Indians, can never look upon England and her Empire with the same eyes as these Englishmen. But if they have imagination they can put themselves in their position and judge accordingly. This they fail to do in most cases and hence their unjust criticism and censure of men like Lord Curzon. They judge an English Viceroy from a purely Indian point of view; it is natural that he should hardly satisfy them. In the case of Lord Curzon, who is thoroughly English and Imperialist to boot, it is very natural that they should not be satisfied with him at all. The Englishman and Indian are so much at variance in their standards and their standpoints. An Indian cannot be expected to feel much for the Empire on which an Englishman sets so much store and for which his fathers have in days gone by suffered so much. Even the so-called "Little Englander" who affects to belittle the Empire feels at heart for it and would resent the slightest injury to it meditated by others. In spite of the cant that is being talked by some on the subject, the truth must be recognised and looked full in the face by Indians that England governs India as part of the British Empire first for herself and then for the Indians.

Nothing in contemporary politics does so much harm as the blinking of this fact by Indians and the consequent confusion of points of view. And none do more mischief than those "benevolent" Englishmen who encourage Indians in blinking this fundamental fact and thus help the confusicn. They are to my mind not the true friends of India or of England either, who help the notion that England governs India solely for the benefit of Indians regardless of her own interests; that when her interests conflict with those of India they must give way before the latter. It is some such notion that Indian politicians have got into their heads; and it is by some such impossible standard that they judge our Viceroys. They consider England to be a purely philanthropic country which undertakes the burden of ruling millions upon millions of subject peoples in a missionary spirit regardless of her own interests. They forget that she has sunk capital, and, what is more precious than capital, the lifeblood of her sons, in rearing her Empire in India as elsewhere, and that she expects a legitimate return from all this, somewhat as a merchant does from the business that has been built up by the firm of his fathers. In all political transactions they are apt to look to Indian interests alone and to lose sight of the fact that England has any interests of her own in India. This is the fundamental fallacy of these Indian politicians and publicists who judge of English Viceroys and their policy and acts, from a wholly and purely Indian standpoint. India for the Indians is their impossible standard of measuring the English Rule, and no wonder that English Rule fails to satisfy them. They forget that India is a subject country, and think that they ought to be on the same level as their English subjectors. They forget that the Indian Empire is a sort of partnership in which the predominant partner is England, and that in cases of a conflict of interests those of the predominant partner must prevail. This is a fact, an inconvenient fact no doubt, but it must be borne home upon the Indian mind. It must be clearly understood by Indians that England means to govern India and to keep it as her possession and that she will do everything that can strengthen her hold upon this country. She is rather shy of proclaiming this fact, but all the same her conduct towards India is based on this. She will not allow anything that tends to weaken her hold upon India.

Now Lord Curzon throughout his career had this one fixed object in his mind: to render India impregnable without as well as within and to eliminate as much as possible the factors that make for disruption. In pursuing this policy firmly and unflinchingly he displeased many and especially Indian politicians. But the task of an English Viceroy is not to please or displease persons or parties, but to do his duty to the Empire and to India to the best of his abilities and according to his lights. If he is so fortunate as to please the Indians whilst doing his duty, it ought to be considered a lucky coincidence. He should not for the sake of pleasing them and gaining their momentary applause, swerve from the thorny path that duty points him. His foreign policy has been much criticised by his Indian critics. But they are not and cannot, in the nature of things, be in a position to judge of it fairly in all its bearings. Even if they had the will, they lack the necessary knowledge of foreign politics which alone can enable them to be fair and well-informed critics. India comes in contact at some point or other of its vast land frontier with three first-class powers, Russia, France, and China, besides two second-class states like Afghanistan and Persia. The ruler of India has to conduct the delicate negotiations which this contact involves. He must have an eye to what is going on at St. Petersburg or Peking, an ear for what is passing at Cabul and Teheran. Much of this knowledge is necessarily kept from the public gaze Action based on this taken under such complicated circumstances is not transparent to the outside world. The Viceroy is bound not to disclose his justificatory knowledge in cases where his actions and policy are criticised freely by ignorant and irresponsible critics. He is like a person who is fighting with his right hand bound behind his back.

No part of his foreign policy has been so bitterly attacked by Indian critics as his attitude towards Tibet and the expedition to that country. It was throughout a game of sheer ignorance and misrepresentation on their part, displayed against a man who they knew very well could justify his policy to the hilt if he was permitted to disclose the real facts, which were, of course, kept a State secret. But enough was let out to make it quite clear that Russia was playing her old hostile game behind Tibet and that she was merely using the weak and worthless Dalai Lama as her pawn to annoy and, if possible, hurt India, and through India, the British Empire. We know to our bitter cost in two Afghan wars what the game of Russia is; and that Viceroy would be culpably wanting in his duty if he quietly allowed Russia to make of Tibet what she had made of Afghanistan not long ago, and use it as a means of perpetual threat to us on our northern frontier. Lord Curzon boldly grappled with the awkward situation which Russian diplomatists had created at Lhasa, and nipped the danger in the bud which would otherwise have grown to large proportions and complications in a short time. By a master stroke of policy he discomfited the refractory little politician-priests, proud and insolent in their ignorance of the outside world, and showed them the true nature of Russian promises of support at just the time when Russia was entangled in a life and death struggle with her Far Eastern rival. It is a pity that our Indian critics saw in all this nothing but a fresh example of England's insolence to weaker powers, and an illustration of might overcoming right. This explains how utterly unfit are such critics to take broad views, especially when the Empire is concerned, and how little able they are to rise above village politics. That Lord Curzon is criticised by such ought to be his greatest praise. If past English rulers had been guided by their views and encouraged by their applause, there would probably be no British Empire in India or elsewhere left to be ruled by Lord Curzon or anyone else.

Turning to internal and domestic affairs, we find Lord Curzon's policy still more fiercely criticised, and even himself personally attacked by the Indian critics. The reason of this will be again found to redound to his credit as an English statesman. They admit that he came out to this country with no hostility to its peoples: one would like to know what English ruler ever comes out with such hostility. Even Lord Lytton, the worst criticised of our Viceroys, is allowed to have had sympathy for the people. But Lord Curzon is credited with no such sympathy during the latter part of his rule. The Indians praised him during the first years of his rule, and there were loud cries of his being the best the most sympathetic Viceroy, about his being another Lord Ripon and so forth. *Nemo fit repente turpissimus*. Yet suddenly he seems to have grown extremely unpopular. But here we must distinguish. Unpopularity amongst the Indian peoples is a different thing from the unpopularity so ostentatiously expressed by certain prominent Indian politicians and their following. One may be extremely unpopular with the latter without being at all unpopular with the former, because the real Indian peoples are almost voiceless. We believe this to be really the case with Lord Curzon. We know from various signs that with them he is not only not unpopular, but so far as they can appreciate him he is even popular. They know that he has stood up for curtailing needless expenditure and for rendering India greater justice than before at the hands of English politicians. They know that he alone of the last several Viceroys has appreciably reduced the taxpayer's burden, and twice within two years has lowered the salt tax, a tax felt particularly by the lower classes They know that although throughout his rule plague, famine, and other disasters have been raging, he has taken very efficient measures for relieving their suffering, and has cheered them by his genuine sympathy.

But with the small class of educated Indians Lord Curzon is not popular. And the real reason of this unpopularity, almost hostility, is not far to seek. It is owing to his having passed the Universities Bill. There are many educated Indians, and the present writer is of their number, who consider it a good measure calculated to do great benefit to the country. But the class which thinks thus is small and, moreover, not an adept in the prevalent methods of political agitation. Indian public opinion is very hard to ascertain. What calls itself by this grand name is a mere travesty. What exists and asserts itself is mere political ventriloquism, the multiplication of the opinion of one individual or class in many ways and forms, in the press, on the platform and even at the council board. Chiefly the educated few voice their opinions everywhere, and by making the most noise create the impression that there is no other opinion beside theirs. They are mortally offended with Lord Curzon because he would not let them have their own way in the vital matter of education. They were very cleverly using education as a means of weakening the tie which binds India to England with the view of finally initiating a separatist movement. Indeed, some enthusiasts have already formed an Indian Home Rule League in England—with all the consequences which such a movement involves. With this purpose they were gradually absorbing the whole educational machinery in the country into their own hands, very subtly and quietly but steadily. Beginning with the schools, they proceeded to the colleges and finally they captured the Universities. These latter have become anything but educational; they are really political institutions engineered by Congress politicians. This has been going on for a long time past; those who keenly observed raised a warning voice long ago. The Universities and colleges were assuming the aspect of similar institutions in Russia and elsewhere, and were being prepared silently to work similar harm to the authorities in course of time. Many Viceroys were aware of this grave menace. But none of them had the courage to take up the task boldly and arrest the menace before it grew to grave proportions. Each of them realised its importance, but left the *damnosa hæreditas* to his successor. Lord Dufferin made some attempts towards the solution of this grave problem. But even he shrank from it. The task was peculiarly ungrateful to a statesman steeped in English traditions, who shrinks from all methods of repression. But unless he is prepared to see the grave of the English connection with India, he is bound to do something to arrest this movement effectually. We can well believe that Lord Curzon undertook this task with no great eagerness. If he had consulted his own ease and popularity, he would have shirked it and been content to let it drift towards some future successor of his. That he tackled it shows not only his courage, but his statesmanship of a high order which refuses to tinker at reform.

By the Universities Bill Lord Curzon restored the controlling power in the Universities, and through them over the colleges, to the State, gently wresting it from the politicians who had usurped it too long. We say restored, for when the Universities were created nearly half a century ago this power was reserved in the hands of the State and for a time exerted by it. But gradually Government neglected its proper function, and, of course, it was willingly relieved of it by other persons we know of. If former Governments had done their duty, that of Lord Curzon would not have been called on to perform this unpleasant task of restoring to the State its proper control in educational matters. The Universities, and the colleges affiliated to them, would not have become, as they are now, the strongholds of Indian Radicalism and outposts of the Congress movement, in time to grow into the Home Rule movement for India. By this Bill the government of Universities is to be in the hands of proper educational authorities and no longer in those of irresponsible politicians who took to education only as a means to their own end. This was enough to make the Indian politicians, who hoped to turn the Universities to still better account in the near future but for this awkward blow to their hopes, the bitter foes of Lord Curzon. They made a desperate attempt to get into the governing bodies or Syndicates of the Universities through some technical flaw in the Bill. But their adversary was not to be thus foiled. He passed the famous Validating Act; and this completed in the eyes of his foes the measure of his offence. They have persecuted him bitterly; they have reviled him, lampooned him mercilessly. But all this did not make him swerve by a hair's breadth from what he thought to be right and expedient for India as well as England. For India would be the first to suffer if the attempt of interested parties were to succeed in changing the educational character of the Universities, making them political institutions pure and simple, using them as machinery of agitation against the Government and the authorities.

A country situated in the circumstances of India at present would gain nothing, but on the contrary would be much harmed by poisoning the mind of the rising generation, which is specially the charge of the Universities and colleges, against British rule and India's connection with England. It was surely not with these objects that they were founded by England; she generously and wisely thought that education would be her greatest support and bulwark in this land of many castes, creeds, and races, that if she could succeed in training the youth in her own Western ways they would sympathise with her and help her in the task of ruling their ignorant brethren. When these objects were perverted, when Englishmen saw that education, instead of being a help was used as a hindrance, instead of proving a uniting bond was used as the means of sowing discord between the rulers and the ruled, there was assuredly time to call halt and to reform the educational system that had gone wrong. Any other country but England would not have allowed the system to go so very wrong, but would have taken in hand the work of reforming it long ago. Nowhere else, not even in countries which boast of the freest institutions, was liberty in these educational matters so scandalously abused. In all well ordered Governments the education of the youth is the special object of State control. The French Republic neglected it for long, with the result that doctrines inimical to its existence were found to be alarmingly widespread, owing chiefly to the priests having had the education of the French youths in their sole hands. At last the Republic was thoroughly alarmed and the recent stringent measures against the Church and especially its influence in education were passed. Every Government has the right to adopt whatever measures it thinks proper for its safety and stability. The British Government in India has assuredly that right, and those who preside over it ought not to be blamed for exercising that right, occasionally even in a somewhat harsh manner. It should not be called upon to look on unconcernedly when its foundations are being slowly and subtly yet steadily and insidiously sapped. That the educational system as it is worked at present is doing this, is my firm conviction, and those who know something of its working from the inside would be disposed to agree with this opinion.

Though I am an Indian, yet I make bold to state that it is unworthy of Indians to abuse thus the magnanimity of England, and to use the undoubted benefits of British Rule to sap the foundations of that Rule. It is not only unworthy, but also disastrously shortsighted and suicidal. For better for worse the fortunes of India are bound up with those of England. Her strength is our strength and we ought to rejoice in it even out of selfish motives. Anything that weakens her and lowers her in the estimation of the world is sure to react on us terribly. India cannot stand by itself; this has been proved over and over again in her past history. She must be taken in tow by another country. If England were to give her up, another power, Russia, Japan, France would pounce upon her at once. She cannot have Home Rule; she is not fitted for it. She must have English Rule or the rule of some other power. That English Rule is better than that of any other power will be admitted in their calm and reasonable moments by even its bitterest critics. It is the bounden duty not only of British but also of Indian politicians, if they really feel for India and if they are really far-sighted, to do everything that tends to strengthen the connection of England with India, and still more to avoid doing anything that would weaken it. Surely he is not a real Indian patriot who like Mr. Dadabhai Naoroji says intemperately: "The British people stand charged with the blood of the perishing millions and the starvation of scores of millions, not because they desire so, but because the authorities to whom they have committed the trust, betray that trust and administer expenditure in a manner based upon selfishness and hypocrisy and most disastrous to the people" ("Poverty and un-British Rule in India," 1901, p. 386); or who, like him, compares the English in India to robbers and stranglers, the Thugs of old: "Let them withdraw their hand from India's throat, and then see whether the increase in population is not an addition to its strength and production instead of British-made famines and poverty." (*Ibid.* p. 388.) Language such as this comes not from an irresponsible individual, but from one who is the chosen champion and mouthpiece of educated Indians, and who, from his position, may be supposed to have well weighed his words and the influence they would have on the rising generation of Indians. What is worse, these Indians find Englishmen in England to encourage them in their wild talk, and set them a pernicious example which they seem but too willing to follow. According to the late Mr. William Digby, the

English connection with India, is as ruthless and immoral as the conquests of those Tartar "brutes," Timur and Genghiz! "If an absolutely impartial judge, with a full knowledge of all the circumstances in each instance, were to place side by side the wrong and human suffering caused by Timur the Tartar or Genghiz Khan, with the mental, moral, and physical misery endured in India during the past fifty years, the ill consequences properly debitable against Christian Englishmen, who have a high place in the National Valhalla, would be as great as those for which the ruthless brutes of ancient days have had to answer to history, and maybe to God!" (*Prosperous British India*, 1901, p. 4.) It is melancholy to reflect that these are the words of an Englishman about his countrymen's work in India—work which, according to a great French thinker, De Tocqueville, is their greatest claim on the gratitude of civilisation.

But diatribes like these of Mr. Dadabhai Naoroji and Mr. William Digby are eagerly accepted by Indian critics, and the books in which they occur are subsidised and scattered broadcast by the Congress. One may ask sober Indians whether this is to continue, and whether the British Government should go on producing as the results of its educational system such specimens as Mr. Dadabhai and his younger followers. The educational system should be thoroughly overhauled if it is to produce such fruits. It may conceivably be fit for a very advanced country with free institutions and strong enough to stand by itself and wise enough to govern itself. India is not such a country. What is meat for one is poison for another. And assuredly the results which education as at present carried on in this country produces, do not bode any good to anyone, and least of all to Indians themselves. Lord Curzon, let it be said to his lasting credit, saw all this, and seeing this he did not sit still like some of his predecessors, but began to take action in the proper direction. He began with overhauling the Universities which had become the stronghold of misguided and mischievous political activity. He has aimed at restricting them strictly to their proper sphere by placing their management in the hands of educationists alone, and taking it out of the hands of those with whom political aims were foremost. A stricter control than now obtains is to be kept by the Universities over colleges and high schools, and care is to be taken about what is to be taught in them and by whom. It may be objected that this is officialising the Universities. Let it be frankly admitted that this is the case. *Res dura et regni novitas talia me cogunt moliri*, may well be said by Lord Curzon in justification. The difficulty and novelty of such an experiment as the introduction of Western education in an Eastern country have compelled him to proceed warily. And the results of this experiment so far, as we have cursorily seen, are such as to make a statesman with his sagacity more than usually cautious.

This is not a question to be decided by the approbation or disapprobation of Indian politicians. In this matter they are, as it were, in the position of the accused. Their disapprobation and denunciation are natural. Until now they alone have had a hearing, and we have heard much of the dire consequences which are to befall the Universities owing to this measure. There is time now, since Lord Curzon's personality is to be withdrawn from our midst, to judge the question dispassionately in the dry light of reason. And we think the judgment of sober enquirers will justify the man and his measure. The Universities are to be officialised, and what of that? Is not nearly every department in India official or officialised? And is not this required by the condition in which education now is and will remain for a long time to come? Does not everything in India, and the East generally, fall within the province of Government? The Congress itself clamours every year that the State does not do enough for this and for that, and for education in particular, that it does not spend enough on this object. It wants the State to do everything for education except control it. They want men, they want money, they want the State to give them more colleges and schools, and even universities. But they do not want that there should be State control over all these. They point to foreign countries to show how much they spend on their educational institutions, and how little does the State here. But they forget that these foreign countries exercise a far more rigorous control over these, than the British Government thinks of exercising in this country. One may recommend these critics to study deeply the Prussian system of education in this connection. India is not nearly so advanced as Prussia, yet there the education of the youth is entirely an affair of the State, and the whole system from the lower schools to the Universities is under efficient and rigid control of Government officials.

The head and front of Lord Curzon's offence in the eyes of his Indian critics lay in this—that he dared to interfere with the license that was raging in our educational system, especially in its higher branches, and tried to introduce the reign of law there, hurtful to no legitimate liberty but, on the contrary, giving full scope to their energies if they want to use them in the right direction for the benefit of both England and India. The irritation caused to them is too deep to pass away soon. But pass away it will one day, and then, sensible men as some of these Indian critics are, they will acknowledge that the change which Lord Curzon has brought about was urgently needed, and is on the whole beneficial to their country. At present they are blinded by their great prejudice on account of this education question, to the great merits of the brilliant statesman who is passing from a splendid career of useful and conscientious work in India to a still higher sphere with nobler ambitions that awaits him, where the experience gained in our midst will be more widely available for the Empire at large whose good he has so much at heart. It is but seldom that England sends out such a statesman with such rare accomplishments to govern India. During the whole of the last century she sent out three or four such, and in the long roll of England's proconsuls in India, the place of Lord Curzon will be beside Wellesley and Hastings, Dalhousie and Canning. Contemporary opinion in the case of all these men was in violent conflict. Wellesley was hampered and hindered at every turn by the East India Company at home, as his great successor of our day has been hampered and hindered by an unsympathetic Secretary of State towards the end of his career. There was a petition from India for the recall of Canning, just as there has been a petition from Bengal for the recall of Lord Curzon. Torrents of unmerited obloquy occasioned by the breaking out of the Mutiny, for which he was not only not responsible, but which would have been averted had the measures* he strongly recommended been taken, broke but could not bend the haughty head of Dalhousie, confident in his own righteousness of the power of posterity to do him that justice which his contemporaries denied him in their ignorance or perverseness. Marquess Wellesley lived to see the Directors of the East India Company, who were ready to recall him in 1804, render him justice more than thirty years later, when they voted for a statue of him to grace their hall, and presented him with an address in which they called him a great benefactor of their Indian Empire. Lord Curzon is still young, and he may live to receive a like tribute of tardy gratitude and admiration from the people he once ruled so wisely and well.

At present he leaves the country under a passing cloud and the sun of his fortunes, which had become almost proverbial, is suffering a partial eclipse. It is some satisfaction to contemplate that the circumstances that have cast their shadow on him are entirely honourable to him. It is only a shadow from which he will emerge unsullied. The military autocracy, in the struggle with which he has been worsted, is bound in the long run to collapse. England cannot long remain in the present state of military hypnotism. The spectre of military inefficiency is haunting her, and she is deluded by the will o' the wisp of army reorganisation. It is only in such a state that she has consented to such an overthrow of the civil power and triumph of militarism as is implied by the fall of Lord Curzon. But she will be soon herself again. Militarism has never for any length of time gained the upper hand in her concerns. The instincts of the nation are against it. The Indian army, also, is assuredly not in such a parlous state as is made out by rampant partisans of militarism. And surely it is an irony of fate that that army should be so much decried for want of efficiency, at just the time when it is least wanted to fight the traditional foe, who has been menacing the peace of India for a century, but who at this moment is lying low and is not in a position to injure us for many years to come; and that the ruler who has done so much to safeguard the interests of the Indian Empire and to render it less assailable from without, in whose time Russia has been exhausted as she has never been before in our time, without any effort on our part, should himself fall a victim to the panic he has done so much to remove.

September, 1905.

---

* This has been conclusively shown in the masterly *Life of Lord Dalhousie* with which Sir William Lee-Warner has recently enriched Anglo-Indian literature. See a review by me in the *Calcutta Review*, January 1905, pp. 164-172.

LORD CURZON AND MARQUESS WELLESLEY.

Lord Curzon has laid down his high post after nearly seven years of arduous work and embarks for England. Exactly a hundred years ago another great statesman laid down the same post after also seven years of hard and brilliant work to embark for England, in August 1805. There is a great resemblance between the two statesmen, both in their outward circumstances and still more in the nature of their work for this country and the empire at large; and we purpose just to touch on it here. Marquess Wellesley and Lord Curzon are exactly a century apart when their careers in India are ended. But what is more remarkable, both were born also almost a century apart, and Lord Curzon is now of almost the same age as Wellesley when he resigned his high post. Wellesley was born on June 20th, 1760, and Lord Curzon on January 11th, 1859. Wellesley landed in India in May 1798 at the age of 38, at which age the present Viceroy landed in our midst during Christmas of 1898. Both have been here for seven years,—Wellesley a few weeks over and Lord Curzon a few weeks under seven years. Wellesley was forty-five when he left India; his successor forty-six. Wellesley lived for thirty-eight years longer, dying at the advanced age of 83 on September 26th, 1842. We hope and wish that the parallel between the two men will be complete in this respect, and that Lord Curzon will attain a similar old age. The bent of both is towards foreign politics, and Wellesley became Secretary of State for Foreign Affairs within four years of retiring from this country. Lord Curzon is likely to enter the Cabinet as Foreign Minister in even a shorter time. Wellesley was originally an Irish peer like his successor to-day. But while Lord Curzon is not only content to be an Irish peer but is one by choice, his great predecessor was in great anguish of mind when the King promoted him to an Irish Marquisate in 1800 for his annihilation of Tipu. In a letter which Lord Rosebery has printed for the first time in his brilliant monograph on Pitt, that great statesman was at considerable pains to soothe his ruffled spirits at this fancied slight and supposed underrating of his services to the Empire in India, by conferring on him the inferior honour of the Irish Peerage. (Rosebery, "Pitt" pp. 211-216.) Lord Macartney had, fifteen years before, declined the Governor-Generalship to which, on his return to England from Madras, where he had been Governor, he had been appointed in January 1786 to succeed Warren Hastings, because his Irish peerage would not be exchanged for a peerage of the United Kingdom. (Barrow, "Public Life of Macartney," Vol. I. pp. 327-330, 1807.) Pitt, a few years later, endeavoured to obtain from the King the highest reward for Wellesley when about to quit India. But circumstances prevented Pitt from obtaining the Garter for his friend, who attained to the honour of the blue ribbon a few years later in 1810. Lord Curzon may hope for this signal mark of His Majesty's favour sooner.

Lord Curzon had not to encounter foes like Tipu and the Marathas whom Wellesley crushed in his day; his generals have no victories like those of Seringapatam and Delhi, Assaye and Laswari, to boast of. But peace has its triumphs more glorious than war, and the statesman just retiring can look back on an equally arduous if less brilliant record of work done in the field of reform. He had to fight more insidious foes than those arrayed on the battle-field. But in one important respect the work the man of our day had to do has been curiously alike to that of his predecessor of a hundred years ago. In the midst of all his internal pre-occupations he has been ceaselessly vigilant over the movements of Russia, and always on the alert to check her diplomacy directed against us in Tibet, in Persia, in Afghanistan. When his rule shall come to be viewed in due perspective, as time advances, his foreign policy shall come out as the most useful of his several works. Wellesley had the same foe to encounter not only at the foreign courts of Teheran and Cabul, but at the internal courts of Tipu, of the Peishwa and Sindia, and of Ranjit Singh. Persia was even then firm in the grip of its northern neighbour, from which the English had slowly to disentangle it by means of delicate negotiations. Sir Harford Jones, and a little later Sir John Malcolm, carried out Wellesley's policy in Teheran, and kept up that kingdom against Russia.

Napoleon was then our greatest foe, and after subduing Russia he used Russian policy and resources to baffle us in Persia, Turkey. Egypt; and in India itself French machinations were rife at the various native courts. The treaty of Bassein with the Peishwa was aimed really against French influence. A similar treaty had before been offered to Tipu, but made reckless by promises of French support, he rushed on his ruin. Sindia and Holkar similarly opposed us with troops aided by French generals and French armaments, and were fortunately routed and compelled to sue for peace. In the north timely alliances were made with the independent courts of the Afghans and of the Sikhs under Ranjit Singh, and the Russian and French menace was successfully warded off. That already, a century ago, the European enemies of England recognised that India was the most valuable part of the Empire, and that they thought even then to wound her easily there, may be seen from the following extract from a memoir drawn up by a French Officer in India for his Government, which came into the hands of our envoy in Persia, Sir Harford Jones. "The power of the English in India is the most precious portion of the British Empire. It equals in extent, population and riches, the first powers in the world; but you would form a very erroneous opinion of its strength or solidity if you should calculate these from her possessions. It is consoling to me to be able to assure you that this source of wealth, so dangerous to our peace and happiness, may be divided and dried up more easily than is conceived." (Castlereagh Correspondence, Vol. V. p. 408.) Wellesley did all in his power to disabuse England's enemies of this notion of her vulnerability in India; and when, a little while after he left this country, Napoleon allied himself with Russia by the treaty of Tilsit, with India as the distinct objective of both, it was by pursuing the policy that he had boldly laid down that the first Lord Minto was able to guard against the danger. In our time, we have found a new ally against Russia in Japan much stronger than Wellesley had in Ranjit Singh and his Sikhs, and in Cabul and Persia. History will reveal what share Lord Curzon had in bringing about this alliance; but meanwhile we may satisfy ourselves with the remark that some such union of England and Japan is shadowed forth in his book on the Far East published more than ten years ago. Moreover, it is a former Indian Viceroy, Lord Lansdowne who is identified with this triumph of English diplomacy.

But the chief resemblance between the two statesmen lies in the fact that both were hampered in their work during the latter part of their careers as rulers of India by unsympathetic and more or less hostile authorities at home. In the case of Lord Curzon, it must be said that this opposition is of much shorter duration; in fact only the last year of his rule has been marked by the partial disapproval of his policy in Tibet, and in the late notorious incident. Wellesley, it might be said, was for a series of years hampered and hindered and even thwarted in his policy. It was not an unsympathetic or jealous Secretary of State or the minister who then carried on his functions, the President of the Board of Control, who delighted in putting a spoke every now and then in his wheel. Wellesley worked harmoniously enough first with Dundas and then with Castlereagh, who successively filled that office in the Cabinet; of the latter's cordial support of him Wellesley has himself spoken in generous terms towards the close of his life in 1839. "Although he differed with me in some points connected with the origin of the war, he most zealously and honourably assisted me in the conduct of it, and gave me his powerful support in Parliament against all the assaults of my enemies. He at once saw the great objects of policy which I contemplated, and which have since been so happily accomplished; and with a generosity and vigour of mind not often equalled, he gave me every aid in the pursuit of a plan not his own, and afterwards every just degree of honour and praise in its ultimate success." (Alison's "Life of Castlereagh," Vol. I., p. 179.)

But at that time and for long afterwards, till 1858, there was associated with the President of the Board of Control, another power, in the end subordinate to him, but capable of making itself heard, and very often obeyed, in Indian affairs. It was the Court of Directors, mostly composed of merchant princes, having a commercial interest in India. They took the narrowest financial view, and showed themselves very often incapable of seeing the great objects of Imperial policy. The grand schemes of Wellesley whereby he aimed at strengthening the Empire, they did not understand and could not be brought to sympathise with. He several times resigned, and was called upon to continue at his post till his high plans should be fully developed and matured. Writing about his resignation to Dundas in the beginning of 1802, he expresses himself thus: "A due consideration of the relation in which I stand towards the Court of Directors, as a servant of the East India Company, and a sense of the propriety of observing a submissive and respectful deportment in all my official communications with the Court, has induced me to abstain from any official record of the real and efficient causes of my resignation." (Wellesley Despatches, Vol. III., p. iv.) And he proceeds to enumerate categorically these causes to his friend. Among these are some which might well be enumerated by Lord Curzon as his own. "The Court of Directors has recently been pleased to interfere directly in several of the most important details of the local executive government of India; in the dismission of persons employed with my full confidence and approbation for the ordinary despatch of business, and in the selection of others, in whom I cannot confide, and whose appointment is entirely contrary to my judgment; and that the Court has plainly disclosed an intention of pursuing a similar system of direct interposition in the future local government of these possessions and in the choice of persons to be employed in the subordinate executive departments of this Empire." The Directors on this occasion pressed him to continue at his post at least a year longer, and wrote to him in these terms: "We cannot avoid expressing in the strongest terms our conviction that the interests of the East India Company will be essentially promoted by his continuance in India for another year for the purpose of bringing to a conclusion the various arrangements; we therefore entertain a confident reliance that the Governor-General (adverting only to the obligation of superior moment which these considerations impose) will cordially join with us in feeling the importance of his stay in India until these objects shall have been accomplished, and that he will in consequence postpone his departure from thence." (*Ibid.* Vol. III. p. xxv.)

But the friction continued to arise on various pretexts, and the President of the Board of Control found it very hard to preserve harmony between the Governor-General and Court of Directors. At length Pitt, the Prime Minister, who had the warmest personal regard for him, had to write to him at the end of 1804 to come away, as things could not be smoothed between him and the Directors of the Company. "Even if you have not already started," wrote Pitt, "what you will learn by the present conveyance of the temper and disposition which prevails at the India House, will naturally lead you to a determination not to remain longer than you may find necessary to complete such arrangements as you may think it most material to bring to a conclusion before your departure. Things are brought to a point at which it seems to be the clear opinion of your brother and of Lord Melville and Lord Castlereagh, as well as my own, that you could no longer have the means of carrying out the Government in a way either creditable or satisfactory to yourself, or advantageous to the public service. It therefore seems to us clearly desirable that you should carry into execution the intention you have expressed of returning home (if you have not done so at an earlier period) in the course of next year." (Rosebery, "Pitt," p. 219.) Lord Cornwallis was expressly sent out with a mandate to reverse his splendid policy, an inglorious task on the threshold of which the weary old man of nearly seventy, who had come out at that age under a mistaken notion of duty, sank into a grave in this strange land just a hundred years ago in October 1805.

A generation passed away and Marquess Wellesley's Administration passed into history; even ordinary people saw it in its proper perspective in the light of events which followed. His policy had a fair trial, after some years, at the hands of his successors, notably Marquess Hastings, and it had time to develop itself and work out its own good results. Old animosities which it had roused died away. A new Court of Directors had grown up in 1841, whose dividends were no longer adversely affected by his policy, and they voted to erect a marble statue of him as "a public, conspicuous and permanent mark of the admiration and gratitude of the East India Company." (Pearce, "Memoirs of Wellesley," Vol. III., p. 434.) Wellesley was fortunate enough to see this day when the Court reversed its own former judgment and passed the verdict of history. Lord Curzon is still young, and we may be permitted to hope that he may live to see the judgment which a section of the Indian peoples has hastily and thoughtlessly passed on his rule reversed by themselves at a later date in the dry light of reason, and his administration of India pronounced by history as worthy to rank by the side of those of Wellesley and Dalhousie.

Barring this small section, his rule has received the emphatic and enthusiastic approval and approbation of all communities, English and Indian, in every town and province during the past three months. Our city of Bombay has been conspicuous among these. In this it is but following the example set by its citizens a hundred years ago. The citizens of Bombay, English and Indian, in August 1805, assembled under the presidency of a famous man whom our city was then proud to call her own, Sir James Mackintosh, a noted Whig, be it noted, and opposed to Wellesley's principles, which he called those of a Sultanised Englishman; and voted him an address and a statue, the latter of which we have in our midst, we are sorry to say, in a very neglected and dilapidated condition. In this address, in which we plainly see the master hand of Mackintosh, it was said: "The British character is not so far corrupted in us that we can pay homage to mere power and greatness. It is therefore with pleasure that we choose this unsuspected moment for declaring our unfeigned sense of the claims on public admiration and gratitude which your splendid abilities and unwearied exertions in the cause of your country have so justly gained for you during your memorable government of India." We cannot do better than apply these words of our predecessors of a century ago to the statesman who is leaving us this week for good. And the parting words in which Bombay men took their final leave of Marquess Wellesley are even more applicable to Lord Curzon to-day. "We are confident that your Lordship will ever find a happiness worthy of you in the memory of your important services, in the renewal of your intercourse with illustrious and accomplished friends in literature, which you have not only liberally patronised but most successfully cultivated; and above all in the performance of those duties, public as well as private, of which the number is increased and the obligations strengthened by your distinguished talents and eminent station, and the active discharge of which is the safest and most pure source of enjoyment which it has pleased Divine Providence to allot to mankind." (Asiatic Annual Register for 1806, p. 75.)

November, 1905.

THE DISPUTE BETWEEN THE VICEROY AND THE COMMANDER-IN-CHIEF IN LORD LAWRENCE'S TIME.

The recent unfortunate dispute between Lord Curzon and Lord Kitchener forcibly recalls to our mind at the close of 1905 the words written in 1883 by Mr. Bosworth Smith, the worthy biographer of Lord Lawrence, in connection with a similar dispute which his hero had as Viceroy with the Commander-in-Chief of his day. "In a country like India," says he in his admirable *Life of Lord Lawrence*, "it is difficult under the best of circumstances—human nature being what it is—for the Governor-General and Commander-in-Chief to pull well together. It is impossible, unless there be an extraordinary amount of forbearance, tact, and good sense on both sides. The discipline of the army is the proper function of the Commander-in-Chief, and it is absolutely necessary, in all questions relating to its distribution, its pay, and a hundred other matters in which he is deeply interested, that the Civil Governor and not the Commander-in-Chief should be supreme. But it has often happened that the Commander-in-Chief has failed to recognise the fundamental condition of his existence. He resents as encroachments on the part of the civil power a control which is essential to its very existence; a control without which India would be subject to a military despotism such as is not tolerated in the most despotic country in the world, not even in Russia. Hence the strained relations which have not unfrequently existed between Governor-General and Commander-in-Chief in India, and which, owing to the strong characters of the two men, were brought into special prominence in the case of Lord Dalhousie and Sir Charles Napier." (Vol. II. p. 309, ed. 1885.)

The strong characters of the two protagonists in the present struggle might will be likened to those of Dalhousie and Napier, and in both cases the *denouement* has been the same, resignation of one party—of Napier, the fiercely stubborn Commander-in-Chief, in the one, and of Lord Curzon, the placidly firm Governor-General, in the other. But the prolonged struggle between Lord Lawrence and his Commander-in-Chief, though equally persistent, did not come to a dramatic issue, and has therefore been forgotten. But it deserves to be recalled, especially on the present occasion, when the question of supremacy of the Civil power over Military authority has again come to the front so acutely.

Mr. Bosworth Smith, has touched upon the subject and has given us the Viceroy's own version of the affair, as contained in his letters to the Secretary of State of his day, Sir Charles Wood, afterwards Lord Halifax. Sir Hugh Rose was a distinguished soldier, and had won his crowning laurels during the Mutiny in his celebrated campaign in Central India. He was appointed Commander-in-Chief first of Bombay in March, and then of India in June, 1860. His military renown was great and fresh, like that of Lord Kitchener who came straight to India from the South African War. He too, had a great zeal for the reorganisation of the Army after the great crisis through which it had just then passed, namely the Mutiny. He carried things with a high hand. Lord Canning, who was then at the end of his rule, allowed him to have his own way. Lord Elgin died before he could make his influence felt. But when Lord Lawrence came out as Viceroy, at the beginning of 1864, Sir Hugh had to count with an exceptionally firm man, whose knowledge of India was not rivalled by any one. Lord Lawrence at once proceeded to check the undue reforming zeal of his Commander-in-Chief and to keep it within bounds. He found this a severe and irksome task; and it produced constant friction till the Commander-in-Chief retired in March, 1865, at the end of his term. For fifteen months this tension between the Viceroy and the Commander-in-Chief lasted, and in every matter, even small ones, the soldier tried to assert himself over the civilian. And it tried all Lord Lawrence's patience and perseverance to keep Sir Hugh from gaining undue ascendancy.

That the quarrel did not blaze forth into a scandal was greatly due to the tact of the Secretary of State, Sir Charles Wood, a statesman very different from Mr. Brodrick. At the same time, he was very firm. Indeed, no Secretary of State was ever firmer. He was called "Maharajah Wood." But he knew how to glove his iron hand. It would seem that once Sir Charles Wood suggested very much the same plan that Mr. Brodrick has actually carried through, in order to put a stop to the wrangles between the Viceroy and the Commander-in-Chief. But Lord Lawrence so ably pointed out its mischievousness that Sir Charles at once withdrew his suggestion. This letter is so important just now that we may well give it here :—

"I certainly see and feel that Sir Hugh Rose and I do not get on well together. I fully admit that there is, and has been, more or less antagonism between the Governor-General of the day and the Commander-in-Chief. I see the probability of great mischief and incovenience arising in consequence of this state of things. But I am sorry to say that I do not think that the changes you propose will mend matters. On the contrary, it appears to me that they will greatly aggravate them. By your plan, the Queen's Officer who would be sent out to India would be War Minister and Commander-in-Chief. He would thus have all the power, all the prestige, all the influence attached to the present office of Commander-in-Chief, added to that which the War Minister as Member of Council would possess. He would work and influence all the details of any important military question as Commander-in-Chief, and then carry it through or report it Home as Member of Council working the Military Department. He would be Sir Hugh Rose and Sir Robert Napier (then Military Member of Council) together. I don't see, for instance, how we could send a Despatch Home which was not in accordance with his views. In a word, by the combination of the two powers the authority of the Military element would overshadow and paralyse that of the Civil power. As Commander-in-Chief, the War Minister would have the same Staff to enable him to carry on the struggle with the Governor-General whenever his views were not admitted." (*Life of Lord Lawrence* Vol. II. p. 311.)

Lord Lawrence suggested as the remedy that the Commander-in-Chief should not have a seat in the Council. "He should be a high executive officer distinctly subordinate to the Governor-General-in-Council. His views and arguments would then all, as circumstances dictated, be put on record, and would go Home bearing the authority and influence which they deserved, and no more. In the meantime, he would be required to obey the orders he might receive. I see no other change which would prove beneficial. We must, I presume, have a Commander-in-Chief in India. A War Minister alone would not be thought sufficient. If it would, I would be willing to try the plan. But then he should be, like any other Member of Council, with no Staff and no Secretariat but that of the Government of India. Whether the present system of a modification, such as I have indicated, be introduced, much must depend on the Officer who is sent out. He should be eminently a resonable man; one who could see and admit that Military arrangements must be subject to modifications in reference to Civil and Political considerations."

The remarks which Lord Lawrence makes as to his position as Viceroy, compared to that of the Commander-in-Chief, will also be found interesting just now:—"I myself cannot see how it is possible to suppose that I can influence a Commander-in-Chief of strong views who is fully satisfied that he is in the right. I do not select him; nor have I any voice in his selection. He has nothing to hope or fear from me. He has been brought up in a perfectly different school. He has little sympathy with my feelings and thoughts. He as a rule does not see the difficulties and dangers which are apparent to me. In what mode, then, am I to work? The Governor-General, nowadays, has no bed of roses, I can assure you! He is beset by difficulties on every side. The unofficial classes have no sympathy with him. Many of the Civilians are discontented. His patronage is nearly all gone. That of the Commander-in-Chief is very great, with all the advantage of belonging to and being supported by a powerful profession. Why, the Governor-General cannot even recommend an Officer for the honours which he may think are fairly due, without the concurrence of the Commander-in-Chief! What, then, has he to support him? Only the sense of honour and duty in his Councillors, and public opinion, which, in this country is, perhaps, more uncertain than in England" (*op. cit.* Vol. II. p. 313).

All these remarks of Lord Lawrence in his letters to Sir Charles Wood, then Secretary of State, have a special significance for us in view of the present situation, so similar to that in his own days, and will be read with great interest. One thing comes out strongly in all these disputes. It is as true to-day as when Lord Ellenborough, certainly not very remarkable for taking it to heart, observed before the Select Committee on Indian Affairs in 1852, that "India is a country in which personal feelings are allowed to have very great weight." ("Minutes of evidence before the Commons' Committee," 1852, p. 233). Personal feelings being what they are, we want a Secretary of State with the tact of Sir Charles Wood.

August, 1905.

THE DISPUTE BETWEEN LORD CANNING AND LORD ELLENBOROUGH.

The harsh tone of certain recent despatches of Mr. Brodrick, which are likely to become historical, has been compared to that of a famous, or rather notorious, despatch which Lord Ellenborough, Mr. Brodrick's predecessor of long ago, addressed to Lord Canning in the matter of what is known in history as the Oude Proclamation of the latter. But we have never seen the despatch quoted in full anywhere in this connection, nor has this curious incident, which though meant as a "snub" to the Governor-General and calculated to compel his resignation, only brought about in a sudden and startling manner the fall of the imperious and tactless President of the Board of Control, been related anywhere with the fullness and accuracy it deserves as a close parallel to what has happened in our day. We have unearthed this despatch in its entirety from the file of the London "Times" for 1858, very rarely to be met with in India, which gives the five paragraphs suppressed in the official copy in the Blue-book; and we give it at the close of this article. We are also enabled to narrate this incident properly with the help of materials gleaned from Sir Theodore Martin's "Life of the Prince Consort," the Memoirs of Lord Malmesbury, and Hare's "Life of the Countess Canning."

Immediately after the relief of Lucknow by Sir Colin Campbell in March, 1858, Sir James Outram, the Chief Commissioner of Oude, issued Lord Canning's Proclamation, declaring that with the exception of only six Talookdars who had remained perfectly loyal, all the proprietary right in the soil of that province was confiscated to the British Government, which would dispose of that right in such manner as may seem fitting. This was judged too harsh and impolitic by many, including Outram himself, who wrote to Canning a letter of remonstrance, without, however, succeeding in bringing about any substantial change. Canning had forwarded the draft of this Proclamation home, and it had been approved by the President of the Board of Control, Mr. Vernon Smith, afterwards Lord Lyveden. But soon after this the Whig Ministry of Lord Palmerston went out of office, and were replaced by the Tories under Lord Derby, who were sworn in on February 26th. This was not known in India for nearly two months, and Canning issued his proclamation on March 3rd. Lord Ellenborough replaced Mr. Vernon Smith at the India Office, and when he first saw the Proclamation on April 12th, he strongly disapproved of it, and on April 18th wrote out and sent to India his celebrated despatch, condemning it in terms, not of grave censure alone, but of studied invective. In twenty short paragraphs he proceeded in curt offensive terms not only to disapprove entirely of the proposed action with regard to the Oude Talookdars, but also to condemn the annexation of Oude itself, just when the English were in the middle of a crisis like the Mutiny. He showed this despatch to none of his colleagues in the Ministry, not to Lord Derby his chief, nay, not even to her Majesty the late Queen. He sent it straight to India without informing anyone. And what was still more inexplicable, he communicated copies of it fully three weeks before it could reach Canning, to certain persons in England. But the climax was reached when he allowed his Under-Secretary, Mr. Baillie, to lay it in its entirety on the table of the House of Commons; whilst in the copy that he himself presented to the House of Lords were omitted, with ostentatious care which only set in relief his indiscretion, those five paragraphs which condemned in severe terms the annexation of Oude, a fact accomplished two years before and whose publication was, under the circumstances, mischievous in the extreme.

This despatch, as presented to the Commons, was withdrawn, but the mischief had been done, as it was printed in the "Times" and was likely to be thence copied in the journals of India when it would reach that country. The "Times" thus commented severely on the conduct of Lord Ellenborough, and it well reflected the opinion of contemporaries. "The letter which Lord Ellenborough has sent out, and which even before it was moved for in the Lords or the Commons, was already in the hands of his political allies in this city, is calculated to counteract the force of this measure (the Oude Proclamation), and go far to paralyse the operations of our army. It is calculated to aggravate the sense of wrong, to provoke the foe to more desperate and fanatical resistance, to expose our friends in Oude to shame and confusion as the objects of our own political contempt, to protract the war, to entail future losses on ourselves, and above all to add tenfold to the calamities certain to overtake the unfortunate people of Oude. Nobody can doubt for an instant that the end will be the same, whatever the political party of the statesmen governing India. Lord Canning's course is the best, the surest, the shortest, and as we also think, the most honest way to that result. Perhaps it may have spoken too plainly. Perhaps its language is political, when the stern warnings of the warrior were rather required. But substantially it is the best and only course, and we don't envy her Majesty's present advisers the use they have made of it to snub the distinguished nobleman who had to preserve our Indian Empire in a season of unexampled difficulty, hitherto with no want of humanity, and on the whole, with very great success." The Cabinet were at first disposed to stand by Ellenborough, and Disraeli, their Chancellor of the Exchequer, announced in the Commons, that the Government disapproved the policy of the Oude Proclamation in every sense. This important announcement of the Leader of the House and spokesman of the Cabinet was, as Lord Canning complained on 17th June, instantly carried by the telegraph over the length and breadth of India.

But the Whigs, who were disunited then, came to the rescue

of their Governor-General, and Lord Palmerston and Lord John Russell patched up their personal differences and brought up the matter for discussion in Parliament on May 14th. Mr. Cardwell in the Commons and Lord Shaftesbury in the Lords moved votes of censure on the Ministry. The former was to the effect that "the House has seen with regret and serious apprehension that her Majesty's Government have addressed the Governor-General of India through the Secret Committee of the Court of Directors, and have published a despatch, condemning in strong terms the conduct of the Governor-General; and is of opinion that such a course on the part of the Government must tend, in the present circumstances of India, to produce the most prejudicial effect, by weakening the authority of the Governor-General, and encouraging resistance of those who are in arms against us." Lord Shaftesbury, the famous philanthropist, bore already then a very high character, and was considered to be above party politics. Disraeli alluded to this in his picturesque manner in his speech at Slough before his constituents. "The cabal, which had itself rather a tainted character, chose its instruments with pharisaical accuracy. I can assure you that, when the Right Honourable gentleman who brought forward the motion in the House of Commons rose to impeach me, I was terrified at my own shortcomings, and I listened attentively to a Nisi Prius narrative, ending with a resolution which I think must have been drawn up by a conveyancer. In the other House, a still greater reputation condescended to appear upon the human stage. Gamaliel himself with broad philacteries upon his forehead, called upon God to witness in the voice and accents of majestic adoration, that he was not as other men were, for that he was never influenced by party motives." ("Annals of Our Time," Vol. I. p. 519).

But a greater personage intervened. The late Queen thoroughly disapproved of Ellenborough's harsh conduct, and wrote to Lord Derby to that effect; and this must be said to have brought about in the main the resignation of that talented but eccentric politician. "When these facts came to the knowledge of the Queen," says Sir Theodore Martin, in his "Life of the Prince Consort," "Her Majesty felt deeply the unfairness and irregularity of the whole proceeding, and the danger likely to ensue from the diffusion of the document throughout India. Meanwhile the sensation created in the political world by the wilful act of Lord Ellenborough, adopted without even consulting his colleagues, very quickly brought home to Lord Derby the consciousness that a fatal mistake had been committed. On the 9th May the Queen wrote to him that while she was anxious not to add to Lord Derby's difficulties, she must not leave unnoticed the fact that the Despatch in question ought never to have been sent, without having been submitted to the Sovereign. "She hopes," her Majesty added, "that Lord Derby will take care that Lord Ellenborough shall not repeat this, which must place her in a most embarrassing situation." But Ellenborough had repeated this conduct, and sent another despatch to India without first laying it before the Queen. But this Despatch was very sensible, and approved by the Queen, though she could not help observing: "It is a great pity that Lord Ellenborough, with his knowledge, experience, energy, and ability, should be so entirely unamenable to general rules of conduct. The Queen has been for some time alarmed at his writing letters of his own to all the most important Indian chiefs and kings, explaining his policy. All this renders the position of a Governor-General almost untenable, and that of the Government at home very hazardous." The soundness of this view, says Sir Theodore, was brought painfully home to Lord Derby and his Cabinet. "A strong feeling that Lord Canning had been most unfairly dealt with had sprung up immediately on the Secret Despatch being made public; and it was felt that the task of restoring peace in Oude had been enormously increased by the language in which our annexation of that province had been spoken of. The Ministry were inculpated, in the general opinion, along with Lord Ellenborough." ("Life of the Prince Consort," Vol. IV. p. 226.)

Seeing all this storm raging, Lord Ellenborough resolved upon sacrificing himself to save Lord Derby and the Cabinet. In a letter to the Queen on May 10th, he tendered his resignation, and then informed his chief that he had done so. This the latter caught at very eagerly to get out of the scrape. But the Queen rightly considered the whole Government responsible. As she wrote to Lord Derby: "The fact of the Governor-General having been publicly reprimanded and his policy condemned, remains the same, although the Government have done what they could to mitigate the consequences of what could not be undone." The resignation was of course accepted. The "Times" remarked upon this resignation in these very strong, but not too strong, terms: "All of Lord Ellenborough's acts show a man not to be left alone, and hardly capable of acting for himself. It was a step of no small risk to give such a man the greatest opportunity of doing mischief at the disposal of Government. But even then, if the man had been watched like a wild beast, or a madman, he might have been found a good servant, though a bad master. Yet strange to say, after all these warnings, Her Majesty's present Ministers appear to have given this eccentric nobleman their absolute confidence. The Chancellor of the Exchequer was quite delighted to inform the Commons that his lordship had sent out a letter censuring Lord Canning's proclamation in every sense. Lord Derby entirely justified the publication of the despatch as a measure of necessity, now the proclamation was in people's hands and also known to be under censure. All this promised at least a fair stand-up fight. But all at once the courage of the whole Cabinet oozes out at their fingers, and we are informed that Lord Ellenborough has been thrown overboard and is now at the mercy of the waves."

The resignation of the peccant Minister succeeded in its object of saving his colleagues. Ellenborough said in the Lords: "To accuse my colleagues of any misconduct with respect to the publication of that letter is to raise a constitutional fiction. I am responsible, and let me alone bear whatever censure may be attributed to the act of publication." In the Lords, Shaftesbury's vote of censure was thrown out. In the Commons, Cardwell withdrew his motion after a very animated debate of several nights. The Tories were jubilant. Disraeli described the scene of this collapse in one of his most striking similes in a memorable speech. "I can only liken the scene to the mutiny of the Bengal army, regiment after regiment, corps after corps, general after general, all acknowledged that they could not march through Coventry. It was a convulsion of nature rather than any ordinary transaction of human life. I can only liken it to one of those earthquakes which take place in Calabria or Peru; there was a rumbling murmur, a groan, a shriek, a sound of distant thunder. No one knew whether it came from the top or the bottom of the House. There was a rent, a fissure in the ground; and then a village disappeared; then a tall tower toppled down; and the whole of the Opposition benches became one great dissolving view of anarchy." Though Disraeli could speak thus to inspirit his followers, he knew better than to think that the Opposition was really so disorganised as he described it to be. Lord Malmesbury, who was Lord Derby's Foreign Secretary and a colleague of Disraeli, thus records the latter's real sentiments in his Memoirs: "I regret the withdrawal, as a vote of censure is like an attack on a man's honour, that ought to be met and defeated, not evaded. Disraeli defends the course he has taken of allowing the motion to be withdrawn, by saying the feeling of the House was decidedly in favour of it, the debate having from the first day taken a much larger view of the question than the motion indicated, and turned upon the policy of the Oude Proclamation and of the Government's disapprobation of the policy it ennunciated." The Ministry of Lord Derby was saved, and had a fresh lease of life for a year, during which it successfully transferred the Government of India to the Crown. Ellenborough, who was then sixty-eight, held no other office till his death in 1871, and had no more opportunity for those blazing indiscretions which were quite a habit with him, and which were the cause of his recall from the Governor-Generalship of India fourteen years before this incident happened.

Whilst all this was happening in England, Lord Canning was lying seriously ill of fever at Allahabad. He knew that since his party had gone out there was greater disposition on the part of the new Ministers to criticise his rule in India in an unfriendly spirit. He had sent home a private letter explaining his Proclamation and its motives to Mr. Vernon Smith, the Whig President of the Board of Control, but it is said this was not seen by Lord Ellenborough when the latter wrote his despatch. The real reason of that ill-considered and ill-natured document seems to have been Ellenborough's opinion that he was striking at the late Whig Government through it, and he thought little of its effects in India. Lord Malmesbury says that it was believed that the Proclamation was sent to Canning from England by the late Government; and he also says that he could not credit it. But

Ellenborough believed it, and hence with youthful rashness, though he was sixty-eight, he penned the despatch, thinking he was scoring over his adversaries at home. That was also the reason why he was in such a hurry to publish it in London before it could reach India, and why he had introduced those stinging paragraphs about the Oude annexation, for which Palmerston's Whig Ministry was responsible.

A short telegram, which is said to be very unpleasantly worded. was the only intimation Canning had received of the despatch. The telegraph was then in its incipient stage, and had been used that very year in a tentative and roundabout way. A lady of his household thus writes of its receipt here: "I am surprised that any one in England could write that Despatch as to itself, independent of the marvellous insult and unheard-of conduct in publishing it. But then no one in England can comprehend the enormous amount of mischief such words will do through the length and breadth of the land. When the mail arrived Lord Canning was only beginning to recover from his attack, and I trust Charles (his Secretary) kept the Despatch back till letters from warm friends could lessen the insult and worry. No one can conceive the work he has done of late—the terrific work." (Hare, "Two Noble Lives," Vol. II. p. 448).

He received many such letters even from his political opponents. Lord Malmesbury, who was in the Ministry of Lord Derby and at the time Foreign Secretary, wrote as follows soon after he came to know of the indiscretion of his colleague. "My dear Canning—I am sure you will believe that as perhaps your oldest friend, I am much annoyed at the events of the last few days. I must by the laws of 'solidarité,' take my share of blame in acts which, though marked with inexcusable indiscretion, had no motives of personal hostility to yourself. I never saw the Proclamation nor Lord Ellenborough's despatch until I read both in the "T mes" of two days ago, for neither came before the Cabinet. I consider that I am justified, although a Minister of the Government that has committed towards you and the country the blunder of publishing Lord Ellenborough's secret despatch, in advising you as a private friend, not to follow the bent which your mind may probably take at first, if it be that of resigning your post. Neither Lord Derby nor any of your party wish it, and the whole country is ready to give you all the credit you merit for having so well encountered the extraordinary difficulties of your position. To resign on a point of party and political honour at the moment when you have all but consummated your work would be sacrificing your future fame to a temporary provocation, which ought to weigh an ounce in the balance. The Opposition are to bring in the subject this week in the most hostile form, and may very likely turn us out; but if we remain in office, I repeat that Lord Derby and the Cabinet are friendly towards you. I told the Queen last night that I should write to you in this sense, and she seemed very anxious that I should do so. You will consider this advice as very strictly confidential."—("Memoirs of an Ex-Minister," Vol. II. p. 118.)

This frank and honourable letter seems to have had great weight in deciding Canning's conduct. He replied to the Despatch in dignified terms showing a firm attitude. "No taunts or sarcasms," wrote he, "come from what quarter they may, will turn me from the path which I believed to be my public duty. I believe that a change in the head of the Government of India at this time, if it took place under circumstances which indicated repudiation, on the part of the Government of England, of the policy which has hitherto been pursued towards the rebels of Oude, would seriously retard the pacification of the country. I believe that the policy has been from the beginning merciful without weakness, and indulgent without compromise of the dignity of the Government. Firm in these convictions, I will not in a time of unexampled difficulty, danger, and toil, lay down of my own act the high trust which I have the honour to hold." (Hare, *op. cit.* Vol. II. p. 453.) Canning remained at his post of duty three years longer, returning home at the end only to die in three weeks.

LORD ELLENBOROUGH'S DESPATCH.

The Secret Committee of the Court of Directors of the East India Company to the Governor-General of India in Council.

April 19, 1858.

1. Our letter of the 24th of March, 1858, will have put you in possession of our general views with respect to the treatment of the people in the event of the evacuation of Lucknow by the enemy.

2. On the 12th instant we received from you a copy of the letter, dated the 3rd of March, addressed by your Secretary to the Secretary of the Chief Commissioner in Oude, which letter enclosed a copy of the proclamation to be issued by the Chief Commissioner as soon as the British troops should have command of the city of Lucknow, and conveyed instructions as to the manner in which he was to act with respect to different classes of persons, in execution of the views of the Governor-General.

3. The people of Oude will see only the Proclamation.

4. The authoritative expression of the will of the Government informs the people that six persons, who are named as having been steadfast in their allegiance, are henceforward the sole hereditary proprietors of the lands they held when Oude came under British rule, subject only to such moderate assessment as may be imposed upon them; that others in whose favour like claims may be established will have conferred upon them a proportionate measure of reward and honour; and that with these exceptions the proprietary right in the soil of the province is confiscated to the British Government.

5. We cannot but express to you our apprehension that this decree, pronouncing the disinheritance of a people, will throw difficulties almost insurmountable in the way of the re-establishment of peace.

6. We are under the impression that the war in Oude has

derived much of its popular character from the rigorous manner in which, without regard to what the chief landholders had become accustomed to consider as their rights, the summary settlement had, in a large portion of the province, been carried out by your officers.

7. The landholders of India are as much attached to the soil occupied by their ancestors, and are as sensitive with respect to the rights in the soil they deem themselves to pcssess, as the occupiers of land in any country of which we have a knowledge.

8. Whatever may be your ultimate and undisclosed intentions, your Proclamation will appear to deprive the great body of the people of all hope upon the subject most dear to them as individuals, while the substitution of our rule for that of their native sovereign has naturally excited against us whatever they may have of national feeling.

*9. We cannot but in justice consider that those who resist our authority in Oude are under very different circumstances from those who have acted against us in provinces which have been long under our Government.

*10. We dethroned the King of Oude and took possession of his kingdom by virtue of a treaty which had been subsequently modified by another treaty under which, had it been held to be in force, the course we adopted could not have been lawfully pursued; but we held that it was not in force, although the fact of its not having been ratified in England, as regarded the provision on which we rely for our justification, had not been previously made known to the King of Oude.

*11. That sovereign and his ancestors had been uniformly faithful to their treaty engagements with us, however ill they may have governed their subjects.

*12. They had more than once assisted us in our difficulties and not a suspicion had ever been entertained of any hostile disposition on their part towards our Government.

*13. Suddenly the people saw their king taken from amongst them and our administration substituted for his, which however bad was at least native, and this sudden change of Government was immediately followed by a summary settlement of the revenue, which in a very considerable portion of the province, deprived the most influential landholders of what they deemed to be their property; or what certainly had long given wealth and distinction and power to their families.

14. We must admit that under these circumstances, the hostilities which have been carried on in Oude have rather the character of legitimate war than that of rebellion, and that the people of Oude should rather be regarded with indulgent consideration than made the objects of a penalty exceeding in extent and severity almost any which has been recorded in history as inflicted upon a subdued nation.

15. Other conquerors, when they have succeeded in overcoming resistance, have excepted a few persons as still deserving of punishment, but have, with a genuine policy extended their clemency to the great body of the people.

16. You have acted upon a different principle. You have reserved a few as deserving of special favour, and you have struck with what they will feel as the severest of punishment the mass of the inhabitants of the country.

17. We cannot but think that the precedents from which you have departed will appear to have been conceived in a spirit of wisdom superior to what appears in the precedent you have made.

18. We desire that you will mitigate in practice the stringent severity of the decree of confiscation you have issued against the landholders of Oude.

19. We desire to see British authority in India rest upon the willing obedience of a contented people; there cannot be contentment where there is a general confiscation.

20. Government cannot long be maintained by any force in a country where the whole people is rendered hostile by a sense of wrong; and if it were possible so to maintain it it would not be a consummation to be desired.

The paragraphs marked with an asterisk 9 to 13, were suppressed as soon as they were inadvertently published in the Despatch as laid on the table of the House of Commons. They are not to be found in the Blue-book (Vol. XLIII. 1857-8 p. 410); and are given here from the "Times" of May 8, 1858.

SIR A. LYALL ON ENGLAND'S RETENTION OF INDIA.

On England's right to hold India and her continuance there, briefly touched upon by me in a previous page, Sir Alfred Lyall has some remarks so full of political wisdom that they may be given here, especially as they occur in one of his unsigned contributions to the famous *Edinburgh Review* (cf. Laughton, "Life of Reeve," Vol. II. p. 329.) These articles of the most philosophic among living Anglo-Indians are valuable contributions to the theory and practice of Indian politics, and deserve the closest attention, which they have not generally received on account of the accident of their anonymous appearance in a *Review* which still adheres rigidly to the rule of preserving the incognito of its writers. I have had the pleasure and the privilege of calling attention very recently in the *Pioneer* (Dec. 23, 1905) to these articles, which I trust may soon be collected in a separate volume by their distinguished author. No contributions to periodical literature deserve this better.

"We are aware that proof of the legitimacy of our government will not altogether satisfy those who question whether it is morally profitable, and whether our retention of the country is for the benefit of the Indian people. But it is most inexpedient, because almost impossible, to argue this question upon the basis of reason and utility. We can only say that the English have incontestably substituted a higher and better condition of existence for the state of things that our conquest swept away, that we have set up a moral standard far beyond that of any other government in Asia, and that the withdrawal of our dominion, within any period that can now be foreseen, would have the effect of a political earthquake shaking everything to its foundations, and would probably throw all Asia into confusion. To go further, and to encourage the disposition that is showing itself in England, and is being imitated in parts of India, of treating the morality of our rule in India as an open question of ethics, will only lead the discussion away into a region of fallacies, illusions, and disappointments. The plain fact of conquest not only silences but satisfies the warlike races of India, who submit willingly and are fairly loyal to a strong and just rule, and who are no mean judges of political realities. But in those parts which have been longest under our civilising processes, where the recollection of what went before our time has been rubbed out of the memory of the oldest inhabitant, and especially in provinces that have no political ties or traditions of their own, there is a natural disposition to follow the example now set by one political party in England, of treating the retention of India by the English as a debatable matter, as a claim needing to be constantly explained and justified ; or else as a temporary arrangement for managing the affairs of India during its period of tutelage.

"Upon this view of the situation we feel bound to remark that, however essential it may be to keep constantly before our eyes the moral purpose running through the existence and conservation of our dominion in India, yet to stake our title to this great possession upon grounds of morality or temporary expediency, is to risk it upon an unstable, because always a questionable foundation. In all settled governments it is a great advantage, almost a necessity, that the supreme authority should be personified in some ultimate idea or institution placed in the common estimation beyond discussion; and from the English point of view this fundamental principle should be the permanency and indisputable right of the Queen's dominion in India. It may be proper for the nation to entertain as a remote eventuality the notion of transferring India to the Indians whenever they become competent for autonomy, and to regard it, in the abstract, as a consummation to be devoutly wished for ; but if this intention be constantly proclaimed publicly and authoritatively, we are very likely to delay and defeat our own ends. For, in the first place, the question as to the precise stage and degree of moral and material progress at which the Government may be safely handed over to the natives of India would soon become a matter of frequent discussion, recurring with increased animation, and causing chronic divisions and uncertainty. Government upon such a provisional theory as this has never yet been intelligible to the greater part of mankind ; and in India, where everything has hitherto rested upon direct authority, to make the right to rule a matter of argument and demonstration would be like the building of the Tower of Babel ; the whole enterprise would break down amid the confusion of tongues. In the second place, although no English statesman would hesitate to grant India all the independence and autonomy that she can fairly earn and exercise under the British Crown, yet we are bound to take heed lest we promise more than we are able to perform, or raise premature expectations in regard to a political future that no one can yet foresee. History affords very few precedents warranting the belief that any country has ever been trained and disciplined from a low level up to a high standard of self-governing capacity and social union, by the deliberate tuition of a superior governing race ; and in a country like India, of vast extent and population, full of manifold elements of discord and disunion, the experiment is surrounded by extraordinary difficulties. That we shall do our best to promote the political elevation and welfare of our Indian fellow-subjects, is certain ; but we are likely to succeed better by encouraging an active principle of amalgamation and cohesion than by pointing to the goal of eventual separation. We must deal with India as with an integral part of our empire, that is to grow steadily into closer connection and common interest with England ; not as with a dependency that is to be schooled up to a certain point and then turned out into the world to shift for itself. To delude the inexperienced Indians with vague promises of setting them up on their own account in political life, as soon as they shall have learnt our lessons, is not political morality. The immense majority of those who listen to such professions are puzzled or incredulous; the advanced party of educated natives, eager and sanguine, do not consider that the reversion of India, if ever we become tired of holding it, would in all probability fall to the Indians, a race supremely intellectual and philosophic, but deficient in the political faculty. Two powerful States, full of energetic and adventurous races, are at this moment overhanging the northern frontiers of India: Russia which commands all North-West Asia; and China which has for ages ruled the richest and most populous regions of the North-East; while on her long seaboard, India, as soon as she is left to herself, will be again exposed to attack from all maritime powers. A country so situated must take a very high degree in the art of political consolidation before it can establish itself as a self-sacrificing, self-preserving commonwealth or federation of States within its natural boundaries. For the present, therefore, the less we indulge in pledges or speculations as to the final outcome of our administration of India, the better it will be for all concerned. If the English are content to declare that they hold India by a just and valid title, and that they intend to preserve and improve their heritage, having the welfare of the people as their paramount object, that is a position plain and profitable to us all. If they propound for academic debate the thesis as to the moral justification of their government, and if they persist in asserting that they only desire to remain so long as India may require their good offices, they may soon get worsted in argument, and later they may find themselves elbowed, more or less politely, altogether out of the country."—(*Edinburgh Review*, Vol. CLIX. pp. 38-41.)